By

On the Occasion of

Date

EVERYDAY

Meditations of a Grateful Heart

ABUNDANCE

TONI SORTOR

BARBOUR BOOKS

An Imprint of Barbour Publishing, Inc.

EVERYDAY

Meditations of a Grateful Heart

ABUNDANCE

Published by Barbour Books, an imprint of Barbour Publishing, Inc., P.O. Box 719, Uhrichsville, Ohio 44683, www.barbourbooks.com

 Member of the
Evangelical Christian
Publishers Association

Printed in the United States of America.
5 4 3 2 1

CONTENTS

INTRODUCTION

Living an abundant life doesn't really have a lot to do with money. As long as our basic needs for shelter and food are met, we are free to enjoy life in its wonderful diversity. It doesn't take cash to marvel at a perfect sunset or join a child in play, as long as we don't insist on seeing the sunset in Bali or playing with the child at Disneyland.

Living abundantly does require a certain type of mind-set, however. It takes attention to the details of life that we often don't notice in our hectic lives. Beauty is closely related to the little things in life, and abundance is about seeing beauty—not beauty as the world generally sees it, but beauty as God reveals it to an open, curious mind.

If we want a good example of living an abundant life, all we have to do is watch a child as he or she explores the world, discovering the beauty of a dandelion or feeling the tickle of a butterfly as it lands on his or her arm.

This book is made up of one hundred examples of the abundant life. There's nothing really heavy in here; in fact, abundance is often a little funny. Since these examples were plucked from my own life, they may not match what you have experienced as abundance in your life, but you can use them as starting points or pick-me-ups on an annoying day. Look for wonder and joy in your life. You will find them all around you.

THE VET'S

One of the cats has to go to the vet's today. She just had her checkup; then we went back to get flea medicine, and now her ears are itching. I wouldn't mind all this so much if it didn't involve getting her into and out of the cat carrier. Doing so requires qualities only found in the Special Forces: infiltration, encirclement, and neutralization. Then there's the effort required to fold four rigid, outspread legs down into the carrier at one time without losing your grip on the cat's body or being seriously scratched.

Cats are not stupid. They must know this is all for their benefit, that they will no longer itch or hurt when it's over and we bring them home in about ten minutes. But still they fight it. They act as if we are trying to kill them when we are actually saving them.

Of course, I'm no better when God decides I am in need of correction or remedy. I fight it every time He tries to get a hold on me and put me where I need to be. I don't want to go—the carrier is small and frightening—so I make corralling me as difficult as possible. Fortunately, God is far more patient than we are with the cats and doesn't use brute force on us. As with the cats when it's time to go home, all He does is leave the door open, and I walk right in.

Do not despise the Lord's discipline and do not resent his rebuke, because the Lord disciplines those he loves.

—Proverbs 3:11–12

PREDATOR

A snowstorm had come in overnight, and our backyard was full of birds at the feeders and squirrels beneath, filling up on whatever the birds let drop to the ground. Every time the wind picked up and more snow blew in, the animals ate with renewed vigor, fighting for any available perch and packing in the food as if the storm would never end. They needed massive amounts of food to keep their metabolism going in the harsh weather. The whole yard was full of flights coming in or leaving, weaving and darting, bullying and being bullied.

Suddenly it all stopped. A squirrel sitting on a deck rail flattened himself to the wood, not even moving his tail. Many of the birds flew silently into the woods, disappearing among the pine boughs; others hunkered down in snow piles, their little bodies shaking. What had happened? I looked into the sky and saw a hawk circling high above the yard in search of his own meal. He made two or three circuits before gliding off, claiming none of my flock. Their awareness and inborn instincts had saved them from the predator this time, and they went back to their frenzied feasting as if nothing had happened. They were no strangers to sudden, violent death. It was snowing, they needed food, and the hawk was gone.

> *"Are not two sparrows sold for a penny?*
> *Yet not one of them will fall to the ground*
> *apart from the will of your Father. So*
> *don't be afraid; you are worth more than*
> *many sparrows."* —Matthew 10:29, 31

FIGHT TIME

My husband and I rarely argue or fight, although we often disagree, but putting up the Christmas tree used to do us in every year. After hours of work and disagreement, we would finish the job in silence, the Christmas spirit noticeably absent. Both of us would spend the next few days sneaking back to the tree to reposition a light or ornament. Finally, after years of Christmas-tree tempers, we learned to do the job in silence, to just get it done before someone erupted. He anchors the tree and puts on the lights while I busy myself in the kitchen; then I put on the decorations while he disappears elsewhere. It's hardly a joyous celebration, but it works for us, and the tree gets done without snarls.

We have no idea why we get so surly. We agree on type of tree, type of decoration, even type of lights. Maybe he's not as precise in light placement as my father was; maybe I don't decorate the back of the tree as well as his mother did. Whatever the deep, hidden reasons, we're certainly out of step when it comes to trimming trees. All I know for sure is that the Lord in His mercy has provided us a system to avoid a yearly fight and to be able to sit back on the couch with our feet up and tell each other what a beautiful tree we have this year.

Let us not become weary in doing good, for at the proper time we will reap a harvest if we do not give up. — Galatians 6:9

GOOD NEWS OF
GREAT JOY

It was December 24, and half the town was standing in the checkout lines at Shop Rite, fully three-quarters of us in foul moods. Why couldn't people plan ahead? Why did the store put in a new credit card system that baffled everyone the week before Christmas? What was that woman going to do with five pounds of broccoli? All I had in my basket were five sweet potatoes, for which I would stand in line at least ten minutes. Bah, humbug!

Ahead of me, a tiny baby reclined in his carrier, which was wedged into the metal seat meant for toddlers and eggs. He was so bundled up his cheeks glowed red. When his eyes met mine, he broke into a full-body smile, his arms reaching vaguely in my direction, his feet thrashing merrily, his mouth making little baby gurgles. "He's so beautiful," I told his mother as I smiled back at the baby, which threw him into even more ecstatic wiggles.

In seconds people from neighboring lines were playing peekaboo, smiling at those near them, totally captivated by the baby's complete and unconditional happiness. Suddenly I knew exactly how the shepherds and wise men must have felt so long ago. "Merry Christmas," I said to the cashier as I reached her.

"Merry Christmas to you," she replied, still grinning in the baby's direction as his mother made her way toward the exit. "Cash or charge?"

"This will be sign to you: You will find a baby wrapped in cloths and lying in a manger." —Luke 2:12

SECOND THOUGHTS

It was mid-January, just about dawn. The sun was stretching, barely beginning to lift its head over the hills to the east. I could tell that much before I pulled back the drapes covering my kitchen window.

What I saw next took my breath away. We had had an ice storm overnight, and the world—my world, at least—was ablaze with diamonds. The horizontal rays of the sun threw every tree branch into sharp detail. Icicles glittered below every mundane surface. Even the garbage cans were works of art. My first thought was, *Wow! Thank You, Lord!*

My second thought was, *Wonder if I'll be stuck in the house all day? I have to get to the store.* The glorious sight outside my window had not changed, but my perception of it had, and some of the overwhelming magic had lost its sheen. I sat by the window to sip my coffee, watching as the rapidly rising sun dimmed some of the lights and illuminated others in a changing light show, but the *Wow!* moment was gone.

Second thoughts do that to us. Our rational minds slide right past moments of glory and anchor us to firm reality. That's not all bad—some first thoughts should be carefully reconsidered—but we need to train ourselves not to let our blessings slip away before we take at least a moment to enjoy them and thank the Lord for giving us a glimpse, no matter how brief, of His glory.

> " *'He is like the light of morning at sunrise on a cloudless morning.' "* —2 Samuel 23:4

OLD FRIENDS

I had a Japanese friend, a pen pal since our teenage years whom I only saw three times in my life when he traveled to our country on business. We were in our twenties on his first visit and in our fifties on his last. Each time we saw each other we would both break into laughter because the other had grown so old since our last visit. He died in an earthquake shortly after our last visit, but I still remember him as the nervous youth I first met, unsure of his English, afraid of somehow offending us without meaning to. He will always be young to me, even though on his last trip he had gone bald, grown shorter, and developed a little potbelly no suit jacket could hide.

I never learned of his death officially—there was no one I could call—but the earthquake was centered in his town, and I saw the devastation on television. It's been years since then, and I have not heard from him. If he had survived, he would have thought to contact me—he was too kind not to. He is still my friend, and I believe we will eventually meet again, if not in this life, then in the next. Either way, we're sure to laugh when we see how old we have become.

"On behalf of a man he pleads with God as a man pleads for his friend." —Job 16:21

TECHNOLOGY

I venture into new technologies kicking and screaming. I learn what I need to learn, but I never enjoy it. To this day, I cannot program a new number into my telephone's quick-dial system, and I break into a sweat when I have to change a toner cartridge. Downloading E-mail attachments gives me great concern. What if I push the wrong button and send an important file off into the universe, never to be seen again?

Fortunately my husband and grown sons are

geeks (I say this with profound respect). They zip around my computer, installing new programs and updates whenever needed. My only complaint is when one of them changes the settings on my desk chair and I find my feet no longer touch the floor.

One day I told my eldest son I had fallen in love with the first computer game I ever paid for, only to find he had been playing the same game for months. We exchanged hints, and while he did most of the instructing, I had found a few tricks to give to him. I swear I saw a little glimmer of respect in his eyes that day. I was still a computer baby, but maybe there was hope for me, after all. I'll never love technology, but it has brought some good things into my life, including something in common with my adult sons, which I consider a blessing.

"Oh, for the days when I was in my prime, when. . .my children were around me."

—Job 29:4–5

DO I NEED
TO KNOW THIS?

I have a theory that the human brain eventually gets full. The tighter you pack it, the more it will leak out old facts, especially as you get older. At least that seems to be my experience. For instance, now that we have grandchildren, it's less important for me to remember my children's names and more important to remember those of the grandchildren, so I have been known to call my son by my grandson's name, or my grandson is suddenly elevated to a son. Something's leaking, you see.

I've become highly selective in what I learn. I fish, but I don't take fish off the hook. Indeed, the guide gets upset if I even try. It's something I don't need to know right now. I know how to use a computer but choose not to know how to attach files to an E-mail. For now, I get away with it. Would you believe my husband wants me to learn how to balance the checkbook on the computer? I can barely do it with a pencil and handheld calculator!

Where's the blessing in this state of affairs? Well, I've been blessed with a loving family that thinks it's funny when I forget their names. My refusal to learn every silly fact that comes by leaves me with time to play with my grandchildren. I'm sure there's no scientific basis for my "full brain" theory, but it's not a subject I intend to research. It would take up precious room in my brain.

Such knowledge is too wonderful for me,
too lofty for me to attain. —Psalm 139:6

DO IT YOURSELF

There are some people who should never pick up a hammer or try to rewire a lamp. If they don't electrocute themselves, it will take at least four holes in the wall before they find a stud and get a picture hung. Fortunately my husband can do almost everything that needs doing. Our son-in-law calls their new house "The house that Grandpa built." That's an exaggeration, but we do get a lot of calls that end "And bring your ladder."

He learned a lot of handyman tricks by

following repairmen around the house and asking questions (you can imagine how much they like that). Other things he picked up on his own along the way and never forgot. His talent saves us a lot of money, but he does know when a job is beyond him and an expert is needed.

I'm sure this handiness is a gift of God, because my husband never studied any of this and works as an accountant. He just picks stuff up and stores it away in the back of his mind. So far he's absorbed small-engine repair, basic carpentry, electrical and plumbing systems, heating and air conditioning, flooring, and heaven knows what else. One warning: He cannot wallpaper worth a fig, but I know a great paperhanger and call him before my husband pulls out the ladders.

> *Every good and perfect gift is from above,*
> *coming down from the Father. . . .*
>
> —James 1:17

EXERCISE

We have a treadmill in the living room to remind us to exercise. Gotta keep the old joints loose and the heart pounding, after all. I break into a sweat every time I dust the thing. Once or twice a week I actually turn it on and do some leisurely walking, but I get bored after ten minutes and go find something better to do, even though I know I need twenty minutes of trudging to do myself any good.

Fishing involves lots of walking and climbing and stumbling around in the woods, but we only do that about six months of the year, and a lot of times we fish from a canoe, which doesn't give us much exercise unless we flip it over and have to swim.

I'm afraid that my exercise is mostly haphazard and accidental. I have to weed the flower beds once a week or chaos reigns out there. It's a long walk to the mailbox (give me credit for not driving the 270 feet!). When my daughter's dog is visiting, I have to walk her or else. You get the idea. Somehow, this type of exercise seems to work. I'm not losing weight, but I'm strong and healthy in spite of myself. I figure if the Lord wanted me to run, He'd send a mean dog to run from or an energetic two year old to keep up with.

Be merciful to me, Lord, for I am faint; O Lord, heal me, for my bones are in agony.

—Psalm 6:2

WINTER COLDS

My husband and I both had winter colds, thanks to a visit from the grandchildren, those certified carriers of whatever germ is currently in vogue. With both of us down for the count, life became interesting. Basically, whoever's medicine was working the best warmed up the soup and fed the cats. We nodded on the couch a lot, sometimes staring blankly at daytime television, sometimes pretending to read. We built roaring fires in the fireplace and kept the teapot hot. Short excursions to the mailbox or store were followed by long naps. We talked about things we had rarely talked about before in the rush of life.

In about three days it began to look as if we would both survive. I began basic cooking instead of relying on prefrozen, store-bought dinners, and he shakily returned to work. We still nodded off a lot and contributed to Kleenex's profit margin for the year. On day four, we were more or less back to normal, except for a lingering cough. On day five, it dawned on me that if we'd paid a small fortune to go to a winter resort, we would have paid dearly for everything we got for free at home—soup, fires, quiet (if hoarse) conversations, long naps, and all the time together we could handle at our age. We'd had a nice winter vacation together, despite the colds. Even a sneeze can have a silver lining, I guess.

"This sickness will not end in death. No, it is for God's glory so that God's Son may be glorified through it."
—John 11:4

CHIPMUNKS

The rock walls around our property are tailor-made for the chipmunks that scurry around, in, and among them. We love to watch them as they go about their business—noisy little creatures that seem to be happy most of the time and are always industrious. Unfortunately Max, the stray cat that adopted us, loves them, too—as prey. He kills them wantonly, leaving their poor bodies by the front door as his gifts to us.

Last fall he was wiping them out of the rock

walls at an alarming rate. How could they survive his constant onslaughts? By the end of the season we saw and heard precious few of them. Would they survive the winter, or were they all gone for good, perhaps moved into new rock walls belonging to catless houses?

Winter was kind this year. We had no snow, and the temperature was unusually mild—apparently perfect for chipmunks, because this cool February morning the rock walls are again alive with them. They are gorging themselves on acorns, saving many to bury among the rocks just in case winter comes back. They are basking on top of the walls in the winter sun. Perhaps the mild winter is allowing them to reproduce earlier and more prolifically than usual. There's no way we can keep them safe from the cat, but I can't help but think that God has found a way to care for them and keep our rock walls teeming with life in spite of the cat.

His favor lasts a lifetime; weeping may remain for a night, but rejoicing comes in the morning.   —Psalm 30:5

COLD - AGAIN

I'm coming down with a cold just three weeks after I got rid of one. My sinuses had just dried up. I was no longer forced to carry tissues in my pockets and was no longer finding shredded tissues in the clothes dryer. This is unfair! I intend to complain to the management. I get one cold a year. I have paid my dues and fully intend to wake up healthy tomorrow morning. Willpower will be invoked. . . . Reason will prevail! I will be healthy.

Fat chance. Even this early in the game I

know I am doomed to another two to three weeks of misery. My husband is already keeping his distance, a grim look on his face. Our health insurance lapses exactly two days from today, and while so far I have no reason to see the doctor, I certainly will have to as soon as my warranty expires. All my appliances work that way, so I suppose I will, too.

But it's just another cold, and at sixty-three I know I should be grateful it's nothing serious. I've had my yearly examination by every doctor in every specialty, and I'm healthy as a horse. Except for my nose, which is already sore. And my sinuses, which make me feel I'm living underwater. And my irritated eyes. I'm just a little ticked off. I have had my yearly cold, after all!

" *'I have heard your prayer and seen your tears; I will heal you.'* " —2 Kings 20:5

ANSWERED PRAYERS

Okay, this is weird. It's been my experience that God does indeed answer prayers. Sometimes it's frightening; other times it happens and we never even notice. In the devotion right before this I was carrying on about the cold I was coming down with, sort of stamping my feet like a stubborn child.

I woke up today without a cold. I'm still a little clogged up, but the improvement is dramatic. Maybe something outside was pollinating yesterday and I was having an allergy attack, not coming down with a cold. Sometimes it's hard to distinguish between the two, and since we had no winter this year it's quite possible some plant was getting a head start on spring. Whatever happened, I'm grateful.

Incidents like this have happened before—enough so that I have learned to think before I pray. While I believe God wants us to pray constantly because He cares about everything in our lives, I feel better if I think through the possible consequences of answered prayers before I speed dial directly to God. While my judgment may be inaccurate or my motives selfish, His never are, so there are many things in life I'd rather leave to Him without putting in my two cents' worth.

I don't know why I was sick yesterday and am well today. I'm just grateful I can breathe again.

And the prayer offered in faith will make the sick person well; the Lord will raise him up. —James 5:15

GUARD

In the winter I played after-school basketball, back in the days when guards were not allowed to cross the midcourt line. I was five feet three. The players I had to guard were usually five feet ten and twice as fast as I was, but the half-court rule gave me a small advantage if I chose to use it, and I did.

I would get between the forward and the net at the last possible moment to avoid the forward changing direction, and I'd let her run into me, drawing a foul shot for my team. That's the only way I could play it: Get in position, and end up on the floor. It was a hard way to learn about sacrifice, but it worked. Soon other guards on the team caught on, and we'd end up with more players on the floor than we had left standing. It was controlled carnage. We won a lot of games, but it required steel bodies. Our coaches always threatened to put the mats down on our half of the court.

I'm glad today's sacrifices don't involve regular collisions with the floor. Sometimes they feel as if they do, but I'm not as tough as I was then. Split-second timing is often necessary today, though, as is team spirit and the willingness to suffer a little for the greater good. My basketball days are far behind me, but their lessons are still with me.

Offer your bodies as living sacrifices, holy and pleasing to God—this is your spiritual act of worship. —Romans 12:1

A VACATION FROM AFFLICTION

Things go wrong from time to time: Pets die; children rebel; money is hard to come by. One problem is enough to turn us into grouches, while problem piled on top of problem really makes us feel afflicted. What did we do to deserve all this? When will it end? When every day becomes a burden, how can we have a "merry heart" and a "continual feast"?

I personally use the "But" technique. I have

a miserable cold and an impossible deadline at work, *but* there are two lonely daffodils blooming at my back door that need to be admired and cherished. Our furnace died, and a late-season snowstorm is due, *but* there's a good fire in the fireplace and food in the pantry. My husband may lose his job, *but* right now our grandchildren are happily building a fortress on the floor with his help.

This is not ignoring our problems. They will still exist after we admire the daffodils, but they may not hurt quite as much. It's more like taking a short vacation from troubles, finding some little blessings to enjoy in the face of tragedy. We can't smile and frown at the same time, so it's best to smile whenever possible. Sometimes it's not easy finding the little blessings, but they are still there waiting for us if we only open our hearts and minds to them.

All the days of the afflicted are evil: but he that is of a merry heart hath a continual feast. —Proverbs 15:15 KJV

"AUTO"

Oh, happy day! An electrical appliance finally stumped my husband. The fact that it also stumped me is no big news—that happens regularly—but he knows about this stuff. Daylight saving time has arrived, so he was making his rounds trying to get every clock in the house in perfect sync. I was sitting at the table waiting for my coffee to kick in when he reached the stove. A few electronic beeps later, a few mutters of concern, and he admitted there was a slight problem: The stove was stuck on "auto."

Well, I never use "auto" so what did I know? If we waited until 8:45 P.M., something might happen, but who knows what? It wasn't an option I wanted to explore. "Unplug the sucker," I suggested. That's my normal solution to all things electronic. If you can't rule it, unplug it. The clock went blank when he popped the circuit breaker and accepted the fact that it was 8:45 A.M. when he turned it on again. "Auto" was off.

It might have helped if we could have found the stove's instruction book, but it wasn't in the junk drawer and may never be seen again, although he swears he just saw it a few weeks ago deep in a file drawer. Until it surfaces, it's nice to know I'm not the only electronically challenged person in the family.

"God has brought me laughter, and everyone who hears about this will laugh with me." —Genesis 21:6

THE GARDEN

My family have always been backyard gardeners. As a child, I used to wander through my grandfather's huge vegetable garden in a state of awe, the height of the corn both fascinating and frightening me a little. He convinced me I could eat a carrot before it was washed without courting death and introduced me to the sweetness of a tomato still warm from the sun.

The first year of our first house I built a garden to rival my grandfather's, even setting up a primitive irrigation system that required constant tinkering. We never bought a vegetable all season and had some to freeze for the winter. The next year we had our first child, and my gardening days were pretty much over. Now and then I would make the effort, but I was too busy to do it right. All I could manage were a few tomato plants and some eggplant, both surrounded by weeds.

Then I discovered perennials. The previous owners of our house had made the bed, so I filled it up with plants that could survive my inattention, added a few apple trees, and it flourished. I'm sure my no-nonsense grandfather would say I was wasting perfectly good soil growing flowers, but how many eggplants can the two of us be expected to eat? My perennial beds are colorful and forgiving, suitable for our age, and they allow me to get good dirt under my fingernails anytime I feel like it.

I built houses for myself and planted vineyards. I made gardens and parks and planted all kinds of fruit trees in them.

—Ecclesiastes 2:4–5

SURGERY

My husband and I have a deal: When our time comes, I go first. This is obviously an unenforceable agreement. This week he went through a rebuilding of his right shoulder as an outpatient—in at 9:00 A.M., out around 3:00 P.M.—or so the plan was. I called in a little after three, was told he was fine, and drove down to pick him up.

While I was on the road, his body rebelled. His blood pressure went up and down like a see-saw, leaving him white, cold, and shakey. If he stayed down in bed, he was fine; sitting up, he was in terrible shape, which is how I found him. The nurses assured me that all he needed was more time, another IV, and another nap.

By now I was shaking as much as he was, but I leaned down and whispered, "Remember our deal. I go first, so snap out of it!" He looked up at me and smiled. The healing power of tender words it was not, but he drifted back to sleep with a little color in his cheeks. Five long hours later he was more or less ready to go home, thanks to the good nursing care he received and his determination to honor our deal. Sometimes it really doesn't matter what you say, as long as you're there to say it.

You have heard of Job's perseverance and have seen what the Lord finally brought about. The Lord is full of compassion and mercy. —James 5:11

ITCH

My husband is recovering from shoulder surgery. He shouldn't move the shoulder for two weeks, so the doctor gave him a harness that makes it impossible for the shoulder to move. All in all, he's making great progress, even though he's bored to death. His main complaint is that everything itches. His stitches itch; the skin under the harness itches; the beard he's growing because he can't shave left-handed itches. We use lotions and powders, but still he itches. It's driving us both crazy. The cat that sleeps on my husband's stomach is not happy, either, because my husband itches in his sleep.

The itching is the least of all possible problems, of course. The surgery might not have done the job. He may not be able to fish all summer. He can't drive. He faces weeks of physical therapy, and he starts a new job as soon as the stitches come out. But these worries don't bother him too much because he has the itching to complain about. In a weird way the itching is a blessing, something that takes his mind off more serious concerns. God knows how easily we humans are distracted and sometimes places irritating but harmless annoyances between us and more serious developments until we are strong enough to deal with them. For now, it's good that he itches.

" I will heal my people and will let them enjoy abundant peace and security.' "

—Jeremiah 33:6

FUNERAL

My husband's father recently passed away after a full, happy, ninety-six years of life. He was a no-nonsense man who expected his children, grandchildren, and great-grandchildren to do the right thing at all times and forgave them when they didn't. The memorial service featured a eulogy by our nephew, an ordained pastor who flew in from the Midwest. I had never heard him preach before and was impressed both by his words and the simple fact that he held it all together while the rest of us could not. His eyes were red, but his voice was strong. Grandpa would have been proud.

We reached the cemetery to discover that the plot for the urn had been opened in the wrong spot and there were no workers available. Fortunately, we arrived before the rest of the mourners. Our two sons, one of whom had worked at the cemetery for four summers in his youth, took off their suit jackets, grabbed shovels, and did what had to be done, like the men they are. Grandpa would have been proud.

Funerals today are often sanitized and impersonal, with professional help doing the hard work and staving off anything that might upset the family, but this one was a hands-on experience, much like those of two or three generations ago. Instead of just standing there, all of our children willingly gave their last service to their grandfather, no matter how hard it was for them. I'm sure Grandpa was proud.

Give everyone what you owe him. . .if respect, then respect; if honor, then honor.

—Romans 13:7

CATCHER

In the spring, when softball came around, I played catcher on our after-school team. I got the job because I was the only one on the team with the leg strength to squat for long periods of time and could catch pitched balls with some regularity. I liked the position because it did not leave me with nothing to do for long periods of time, as playing the field would. It's also the only position where you can see everything that's going on, and at our skill level, it was a good idea to know where the ball was at all times.

In time, I discovered that being a softball catcher was good preparation for motherhood. I had great peripheral vision—eyes in the back of my head, the kids thought. I had the leg strength to keep up with three toddlers at once. I learned to position myself so I could see whatever was going on, and being a mother was certainly never boring.

I sometimes wonder if former outfielders still watch airplanes when they should have their eyes on something else. Do pitchers still forget to duck hit balls? Do first basemen still have the reflexes to make saving stretches while keeping one foot firmly on base? You never know when some "useless" skill will save the day years from now.

> *But to each one of us grace has been given as Christ apportioned it.*
>
> —Ephesians 4:7

LAUNDRY

In our house, a piece of laundry takes about four days from start to finish. The first day it's run through the washer and drier. The second, it sits in the drier developing the proper number of wrinkles. The third day I reheat and fold it. The fourth day it's put away. That's assuming I haven't run out of something vital or created a roadblock by washing more than one load a day, in which case folded laundry piles up, and the cats sleep on it, requiring a second run through the washer and drier.

I don't normally procrastinate in life's little chores. Papers never pile up on my desk. I have a mental "to do" list and enjoy working my way through it, but somehow laundry always sinks to the bottom of my list. We adapt. I can wear a pair of jeans for two days, if necessary. My husband has discovered he can wear a bathing suit under his business suit when all else fails, since he would not think of buying a week's worth of anything at once.

Things are not going to change, laundry-wise. Now that the kids are gone, so is my motivation. Not doing laundry frees up time to read a book, visit the grandchildren, go fishing, or even take a nap. I love laundry simply because I can always put it off without guilt for another day.

There is a time for everything, and a season for every activity under heaven.

—Ecclesiastes 3:1

TEACHER

It wasn't until I tried teaching that I truly came to admire teachers. I was the worst teacher I ever met, a world-class incompetent, so I quit before anyone got wise and fired me. The kids and I had a great time, and I enjoyed being with them, but I doubt they learned anything useful. Certainly they learned nothing in the curriculum.

I had never taken an education course in college because I believed they were a waste of time, and I had no intention of becoming a teacher until someone offered me the job. I had little to no patience as a teacher and spent most of that semester just trying to keep order in the classroom. What I tried to teach they had no interest in learning, and I didn't blame them in the least. They were good kids; I was a terrible teacher.

But I learned a lot. That semester was my first education in failure. What appeared to be an easy job with good hours was in no way easy. I worked hard and long and still failed—something I had never done before in my life and never expected to do. It was a good lesson in humility for a new college graduate who believed a degree could open any door. It might open doors, but it didn't guarantee success—especially when I chose the wrong door to open.

> *Even as he walks along the road, the fool lacks sense and shows everyone how stupid he is.* —Ecclesiastes 10:3

LITTLE CHEATS

My grandchildren cheat at games. My parents had no mercy when it came to games: You obeyed the rules as written on the box or the game was over. The same went when playing with other kids, unless the rule change was accepted by all the players. But my grandchildren change the rules at will when they are losing.

This is a generational issue. When my kids were young, I let them cheat—just a little. Half the fun of the game was looking away from the board and seeing how it had changed when I looked back. Although I never threw a game, I rooted for them to win. That was my job as a loving parent.

Now I'm older and wiser. I know that losing fairly is better than winning unfairly and believe kids need to learn this. I show no mercy and allow no rule changes. If they really need to win every game, they can play their parents, whose duty it is to lose. But if they take their chances playing by the rules and beat me, they have really won something. They cry foul and demand I play like their parents, but I hold fast. I guess this is okay— they keep coming back for more and now and then actually win a game on their own merits.

"Surely the righteous still are rewarded."

—Psalm 58:11

ADULT CHILDREN

Our daughter, the eldest of three, will be thirty-seven this week. She says thirty-seven doesn't bother her but admits she's not looking forward to forty. Since she looks more like twenty-seven than thirty-seven and works out daily in the gym, I doubt forty is going to bother her very much, either.

It bothers my husband and me, though. You can't fool yourself into thinking you have the mind and body of a forty-five year old when your child is thirty-seven. Your fingers don't ache when you're forty-five, and you don't make those little grunts when you haul yourself off the couch at the end of the evening. It's not her being thirty-seven that bothers us, it's us being in our sixties.

I can't really remember being that age. The kids outnumbered us then, and life was constant motion, one big blur of activity and responsibility that went on and on, seemingly forever. It was fun at the time, but exhausting. I don't think I could survive those years again. I watch my daughter taking the kids to sports, running a Girl Scout troop, walking the dog three times a day, going to parent-teacher conferences, baking Christmas cookies, cleaning and polishing endlessly, and I can't help but think, *Better you than me, kid!* It might bother me that I have a child of thirty-seven, but they couldn't pay me enough to be that age again.

Then our sons in their youth will be like
well-nurtured plants, and our daughters
will be like pillars carved to adorn a
palace.   —Psalm 144:12

SUNDAY DINNER

Before we had children, or B.C. as we call it, we went out for Sunday dinner after church. We went anywhere we chose, ate whatever we fancied, and the bill was never more than a total of twenty-five dollars (sometimes the good old days were really good).

When our daughter was born, we switched to Howard Johnson's because they had soft-boiled eggs on toast twenty-four hours a day, and that's all she wanted. A few years later we took her to a real restaurant again, only to discover she loved snagging "lobits" off our plates and soon began ordering it for herself (yes, a four year old can handle a whole lobster with no problem). It was cute but getting expensive. As soon as our first son was reasonably civilized, she taught him to order "lobits" at any and all restaurants, and our fancy dining days were over.

Fortunately, fast food appeared with the birth of our second son, but by then they outnumbered us, and child number three was beginning to think lobster looked pretty good to him, too. We switched to take-out on Sundays.

Now we are again free to dine in luxury if we so choose, but we don't. Our grandchildren are fast food fans, and we prefer to take them where they are happiest, but believe me, I would dearly love to take them out and feed them lobster, just to get back at our daughter!

Better a meal of vegetables where there is love than a fattened calf with hatred.

—Proverbs 15:17

AN ABUNDANT CHILDHOOD

We were pretty poor when I was a child, but I didn't know that until I was a teenager and someone told me. I knew both my parents worked, and our cars were always at least secondhand, and if I wanted spending money I had to work for it, but I was never hungry, and our apartment was always clean (partly because I helped clean it to earn some spending money).

All the kids in our neighborhood played

together, the rich and the poor, running from yard to yard in contests of make-believe or playing baseball in the empty lot. We played outside in all weather until our faces went numb or we needed a snack of cereal or apples to keep us going. We took care of one another the best we could, considering our somewhat barbaric nature, and there was aways an adult available when one was needed, but basically we were on our own until dinnertime or darkness, whichever came first.

Life was simple. The strongest ruled with compassion, although the smartest made most of the rules. The weakest were allowed their turn, and nobody knew or cared what their parents made. If you had fifteen cents for a cola and glazed donut, you were rich enough. If you didn't, someone would share with you. If we were reasonably cautious, we were always safe, and any danger we met was of our own making, not from the world around us. We lived truly abundant lives as children.

"A man's life does not consist in the abundance of his possessions." —Luke 12:15

INHERITANCE

Once grandchildren come onto the scene and their personalities begin to emerge, grandparents face a new and difficult responsibility: their genes, over which they have absolutely no control. They can't say, "I bequeath this one my smile and that one my patience." Besides, the good things grandchildren inherit from grandparents are seldom mentioned. It's the bad traits we are responsible for!

A grandparent can walk into the house in the

midst of a two year old's temper tantrum and be told, "Junior sure has your temper!" The temptation is to say, "No, it's *your* temper, and we knew how to deal with it, while you obviously don't." That's not an option. It's a temptation but not an option if you want to see your grandchildren on a regular basis. The wise grandparent will smile and silently accept the responsibility, knowing full well that the tables will be turned on their children in twenty years or so.

There is another set of grandparents, though. How much can you pawn off on them? If you accept responsibility for passing on your temper (although it is really not your fault, and they should mention their aunt Matilda), will they accept responsibility when the grandchild acts up in school? Not likely. Joint grandparents are better off ignoring their bad genes totally and concentrating on their overlooked good ones that produced the enchanting, intelligent grandchildren they all love to distraction.

I have been reminded of your sincere faith,
which first lived in your grandmother Lois

and in your mother Eunice and, I am persuaded, now lives in you also.

—2 Timothy 1:5

REALITY

Someone made me have my picture taken today. I could have refused, but I was in a good mood (note the was), so I said I would do it. My husband got out his new digital camera, reread the directions, and in fifteen minutes the photo was on its way from our computer to theirs. Instant ugly.

The problem is, I really had to look at all the pictures to choose the best of the bunch. Usually I look at other things in our pictures—kids, dogs, cat, fish—never at myself. But there I was in close-up, every wrinkle showing, my hair flat, and my smile crooked. I don't deny that's how I usually look to the world—I'm not delusional—but that's not how I think I look. Inside, I'm still somewhere in middle age, so my mental picture is younger than the person in the photo. A lot younger. Thinner, too.

Even worse, I know there's not much chance that things will look better in the next picture. No matter how much I diet or exercise, those wrinkles are there to stay. So it's time to update my mental image, to admit I am the grandmother in the photo and be grateful that I've reached this age. I'm not young anymore, but God still loves me, and so do my family and friends.

The glory of young men is their strength, gray hair the splendor of the old.
—Proverbs 20:29

DINNERTIME

I spent twenty years teaching our children the basics of "healthy" dinners—meat, starch, vegetable, and dessert. If there wasn't a vegetable on their dinner plates they were destined for malnourishment, and in my eyes it would have been my fault if their teeth fell out. Of course, the rules of nutrition have changed since then, but who can be faulted for following the example of their parents?

Now I know that balanced meals are only part of good nourishment. Dinner was served at a specified time, and attendance was mandatory, with few exceptions. Dinnertime was our only chance to touch base with one another and relate as a family. We avoided disciplining or preaching at the table—dinnertime was for telling stories, asking and answering questions, and having a good laugh. Guests were welcome and plentiful, if I was given enough notice to peel another potato.

Everyone's on their own now, but they still tell stories about those dinners: how one child hid her peas under her mashed potatoes while another fed them to the dog; how another spilled his glass of milk every day for two years running, no matter where I placed it on the table; how dangerous it was to ask Dad a question about science unless you wanted to hear a fifteen-minute dissertation. Dinnertime provided a lot more vital to good health than vitamins.

> *"You will have plenty to eat, until you are full, and you will praise the name of the Lord your God, who has worked wonders for you."*
> —Joel 2:26

DRIVING CLASS

For the next two days, from 1:00 P.M. to 5:00 P.M., I will be sitting in the public library taking a defensive driving class. Our insurance agent will take 10 percent off our premium if we obtain our certificates of completion. It's a fair deal, but I don't want to go. I've never had a ticket or accident in my life, and eight hours is a large chunk of time. I'm afraid I might fail the test.

It's not that I think this class is a bad idea. It's a good one—for all the *other* people on the road. The only time my driving ability is questionable is when I have to back up, and I go to great lengths to avoid doing that. Sometimes I get a little sleepy when driving long distances, too. My night vision is getting poor, but I rarely drive at night. Will stuff like that be covered, or will I have to learn—again—how to control my car in a spin (in an area where we have one or two inches of snow or ice a year).

New experiences can be slightly frightening and irritating as we age. Things have gone well enough so far; why mess with success? What if I fail the test? Okay, I'll go, even though I don't need this class and will go bonkers sitting on a hard metal chair for eight hours. But what if I fail the test?

Update: There was no test!

Let the wise listen and add to their learning, and let the discerning get guidance.
—Proverbs 1:5

DOWNSIZED

My husband has been downsized so often that it's a wonder he doesn't need a booster seat at the diner. We'll be okay. After a few weeks or months something will come along, and life will return to normal—which in my opinion means he'll be out of the house for long periods of time. Until then things may be a little rocky. I don't handle change well, and he doesn't handle forced leisure any better.

For example, the high point of my day is often picking up the mail and sorting it (a sad comment on anyone's life). Now he handles the mail, and I lose out on the almost-Christmas fun of finding one piece of first class mail in ten pounds of catalogs. Since he no longer has fellow workers to explain things to, I am receiving far too much information for my brain to process. I've stopped listening when his voice turns instructive.

On the other hand, he's been watching me cook and now knows how to prepare a decent pot of coffee (an accomplishment for a tea drinker). He takes the cats to the vet. He goes on-line and tells me what's on prime-time television and how bad the weather will be for the next five days. Sometimes I even begin to think it's nice to have him around the house. Then I realize that he's old enough to retire for good and rush out to buy every paper in the area, hoping the next job comes along before we kill each other!

However, each one of you also must love his wife as he loves himself, and the wife must respect her husband.

—Ephesians 5:33

PETS

Our house always resembled a zoo when our children were young. We had dogs and cats and short-lived fish. The place was a mess anyway, so muddy footprints were no big deal. When everyone grew up, I declared, "No more pets. If you want them, get your own." When the last cat died, I relished the peace and quiet. There was no more fur on my black slacks, no more pet food scattered around the kitchen. I didn't have to break up cat fights at three in the morning. It was so peaceful and quiet that two days later I adopted a kitten. A year later, a tomcat adopted us. So much for no more pets.

I have held out against dogs, however. You don't have to walk a cat, and they do fine if you leave them food and go away for a weekend. Any yearning for a dog is satisfied by borrowing our daughter's dog—our "granddog"—who loves us to distraction and reminds me why I don't want a dog around full time.

I'm thankful for the pets we have had. They taught our children responsibility. They taught them how to love and be loved. They taught them how to grieve the loss of a loved one. I'm glad our grandchildren have a pet I can borrow when I need something furry and our cats are off exploring the world in their self-centered way. But when the cats die, that's it. No more pets. Or so I say now.

For everything God created is good, and nothing is to be rejected if it is received with thanksgiving. —1 Timothy 4:4

GRANDCHILDREN

I loved it when our children were young. I've never been so tired or had as much fun. Then they became teenagers. We all survived those years of growing separation and are now friends, but there were some lonely years when they went their own ways. We would sometimes wish we had more children, until we came to our senses. We were too old to go through all that again. Then the Lord blessed us with grandchildren.

Suddenly we are wise again, loved just because

we're there. I'm sure they feel we are a bit odd, and I occasionally catch them giving each other meaningful glances that seem to say, "They're old. We must be patient with them." Nevertheless, they listen to my husband's old stories with fresh ears, begging tales of what their mother did when she was young (especially when she misbehaved). Their little legs walk as slowly as our old legs, and their fresh eyes see things we have ignored for years. We borrow our grandchildren and spoil them rotten, leaving their parents to straighten them out when we return them full of junk food and thinking the world revolves around them.

Not only do we need our grandchildren, they need us, too. They need our unconditional love and approval. They need to feel they could never disappoint us. They need an extended family that pronounces them worthy and good, no matter what they do. They are our job, our pleasure, our blessing in old age.

Children's children are a crown to the aged.
—Proverbs 17:6

FRIENDSHIP

No one seems to have time for friendship these days. Everyone is over-scheduled, and if there's one thing friendship requires, it's time. You have to invite prospective friends over for an evening before you even know if they are prospective friends. If you seem compatible, you have to keep investing time to allow a friendship to blossom. Finding a friend is as challenging as finding a spouse.

There are also various levels of friendship to consider. Casual friendships are easy. They are pleasant to spend an evening with, go to week-end events with, and catch up on local gossip with. But these are superficial friendships and soon die if someone moves away or their children transfer to a different school. They're like a nice dessert, but they aren't very enriching.

Then there are serious friendships that can endure anything, forgive everything. These are few and hard to find. They may grow from casual friendships but most likely do not because of the huge investment they require. Once acquired, friends like these are precious blessings. You can call these friends at 3:00 A.M., and they will be there for you. In times of tragedy, they will listen to you cry and cry with you. In good times you will want to share your joy with them, and your happiness will make them happy. Good friends are good nourishment for the heart and soul. Take the time needed to build such friendships, and you will never be lonely again.

> *"I have called you friends, for everything that I learned from my Father I have made known to you."* —John 15:15

THREE BEDS, THREE BATHS

I would not go so far as to say this house saved our marriage, but it certainly eliminated a small source of friction. All our married life, my husband and I have shared a bathroom, which meant he got to shower first because his commute was longer than mine. Add to that the fact that he takes longer to brush his teeth than I do to shower, shampoo, and dry off, and you can see the possibility of conflict. He's a bath hog.

But this house has three bedrooms and three baths: one bath for him, one for me, one for guests. The two main baths needed updating—metallic aqua wallpaper and blue tile left something to be desired—so we each chose our own tile and fixtures and paint. Peace reigns! No more quibbling about who folds used towels and who doesn't. No more territorial claims over the skimpy shelves in the medicine cabinet. We don't even have to wonder whose hair is in the sink anymore.

Not that sharing a bath ever put much strain on our marriage. We're reasonable adults. Occasionally I might mutter "bath hog" on a day I had to get moving early and he was still in the process of shaving. Sometimes he would straighten out all the towels while shaking his head. But having our own private baths has smoothed our mornings out. It was worth the two weeks of plaster dust in our teeth.

Refrain from anger and turn from wrath;
do not fret—it leads only to evil.

—Psalm 37:8

THE POND

I know a pond in Maine, a picture-perfect pond surrounded by a 150-year-old forest that has never been logged and never will be. No roads go near this pond; no power boats are allowed on it, and only once were other people there with us. To get to it, you need to fly in, and the pond is so small that flying in can be a hair-raising experience.

Besides being beautiful, the pond is silent. We whisper when we're there, just as we whisper in church. The pond is so quiet that the sound of a falling tree seems to echo forever off the surrounding mountains; loons complain if they hear a small airplane passing overhead.

I have never caught a fish in that pond, although others do, but I go there every year just to soak up the peace the pond offers, maybe to take a nap as we drift silently from shore to shore in the sun. There's a little log cabin on the shoreline where we could spend the night if we wanted to or had to, but I don't want to stay there. Doing so—cooking and sleeping and laughing—would somehow make the pond less special, bringing the real world into what I consider an earthly paradise. Still, a fish now and then might be nice.

For the kingdom of God is not a matter of eating and drinking, but of righteousness, peace and joy in the Holy Spirit.

—Romans 14:17

HEALTH

I just had my annual mammogram (any women over the age of forty may feel free to groan). While it's still not something to look forward to, they've made mechanical improvements, and the whole thing is much easier. Two months ago I had my annual flu shot, so now I'm healthy while everyone else is coughing. My eye doctor assures me that my failing eyesight is just old age and will be correctable for years to come, and my internist says those little irregular heartbeats are perfectly harmless although annoying.

On the other hand, one of my grandmothers died in the flu epidemic of 1918. The other died equally young from a heart attack, while my great-grandmother went blind in middle age. Longevity does not run in my family, yet I am still as healthy as a horse, thanks to my collection of doctors. Every time I have to change insurance plans and find a whole new set of doctors, I try to be thankful that I have insurance at all and the health system is doing far better for me than it did for my ancestors.

Good health is a great blessing, even if maintaining it is often a pain in the neck. Yes, the health system is still full of inequities and in need of improvement, but the older I get, the more I appreciate it, especially since my ancestors rarely survived long enough to qualify for Medicare.

" 'But I will restore you to health and heal your wounds,' declares the Lord."

—Jeremiah 30:17

COYOTE

I knew we had coyotes in the area when a town to the north began losing its cats at an alarming rate. They went out and never came back. Then I saw her early one morning out the window. She skulked across my backyard from her nighttime hunt, on her way into the small area of woods by the creek. My cats were both inside, so I watched her without fear. Skinny, obviously hungry, she paused to glance at me then hurried off, never to return.

She was probably driven into our suburban

area by development to the north. Once again man encroached, and the animals retreated, but not without complaint. She must have been very hungry to risk being seen here—maybe she had pups to feed. As wonderful as it was to see her, she didn't belong here, and I held out little hope that she would survive. She was meant to live in the wild, not in a suburban area. She would find little mercy here in her exile.

Still, I was grateful for my close-up look at her, so I asked the Lord to bless her and keep her, maybe show her a place she could live in safety, if it was His will for her. She had shown herself to me, paused and looked me in the eye, creature to creature. The least I could do was to wish her well.

And God said, "Let the land produce living creatures according to their kinds: livestock, creatures that move along the ground, and wild animals."

—Genesis 1:24

THE SWING SET

Our backyard came with a swing set consisting of two sandboxes, a slide, one swing, and a plywood fort. It was old and ugly, but we left it out back for the grandchildren to enjoy. Finally we realized they weren't playing on it, so we tore it down. Mistake. For weeks they didn't even notice it was gone, but one day Allie stormed in, demanding to know what we had done with her swing set. Believing honesty is always best, we pointed to the remains in the woodpile and explained its demise.

She mourned the swing set for a month or so, standing by the site and shaking her head at the wanton destruction of something she had never taken any interest in. She would give me baleful looks and kick the two surviving sandpiles, useless reminders of what was once her swing set.

If I had it to do again, I would leave the swing set where it was, ugly and unused or not. I didn't think she would care, but she did. I have since been forgiven. I know this because she made me a huge sand cake with a stick candle on my birthday. When the dog destroyed it, she made me another so I could blow out the "candle." Her forgiveness was the best present I got all day. Believe me, those two sandpiles will stay exactly where they are until she graduates from college!

Blessed is he whose transgressions are forgiven, whose sins are covered.

—Psalm 32:1

GROUNDHOG

If I had not been sitting by the kitchen windows, I would never have seen him, but the grass was two weeks' tall and definitely rippling across the yard at a pretty good pace. In my experience, grass doesn't move like that, so I watched it carefully until I spotted what looked like a moving rock heading from the woodpile to the woods. When it reached the rock wall, it paused, hauled itself up onto the wall, then moved into the trees. Groundhog. I'd seen enough of them by the edge of roads but had never seen one in my own suburban backyard.

The groundhog has been with us every summer since. I see no reason to capture him. Where would I put him—in a neighbor's yard? He only seems to destroy the lupines, which aren't very happy here, anyway. He's my excuse for not planting a vegetable garden I would have to weed and water, and he seems to be a lone bachelor, so we're not about to be overrun with groundhogs.

Twice a day he makes his way across my yard, sometimes boldly, sometimes pretending to be a moving rock. If I see him eyeing any perennials, I go out and tell him to move on, but other than that, he's welcome to hang out in the woodpile as a seasonal guest.

> *"And to all the beasts of the earth and all*
> *the birds of the air and all the creatures*
> *that move on the ground—everything that*
> *has the breath of life in it—I give every*
> *green plant for food."* —Genesis 1:30

THUNDERSTORM

When I was young, my father would wake me up and lead me to the porch to watch thunderstorms. He never said much beyond "Don't worry. It's safe here," but that was enough to ease my fears and enable me to enjoy the wildness spreading out before us and tearing at our hair. He taught me to compute our distance from each bolt of lightning, and if I didn't like the results he would laugh and reassure me. He taught me exactly what natural factors produced thunder and lightning, but most of the time we simply stood there in silence and let the glory roll over us and envelop us in awe.

My father was not a religious man, but he did understand power and glory. He called it nature. I accepted that, within nature's limits, but knew it was somehow more than nature, unless you broadened that term to include anything that couldn't be explained. We didn't argue about religion, though. I couldn't change his mind, and he allowed me the dignity of my own beliefs.

There weren't many things we agreed on as I grew up, but every time a thunderstorm rolled in, we'd meet on the front porch, just the two of us, and laugh as the thunder shook us to the bone and the lightning made spots dance in our eyes. Whatever we individually attributed it to, it was one awesome light show!

> *"How faint the whisper we hear of him!*
> *Who then can understand the thunder of*
> *his power?"* —Job 26:14

DOORS

What is it with cats and doors? My cats allow no interior door to be shut, just in case a cat napping in the kitchen sun has an urgent need to go nap on a bed. Any overnight guest who decides to shut a bedroom door is in for noisy, indignant yowls guaranteed to keep them awake until we grab the offended cat and put him outside for the night. That, of course, involves more doors and more indignity.

Our cats also hold me personally responsible for the weather, which causes more door problems.

Max, the indoor-outdoor cat, will charge out the front door with enthusiasm, suddenly realize he's getting wet, and yowl to come back in. Within two minutes he will ask to go out the back door, and heaven help me if it's raining in the backyard, too! Tillie, the indoor cat who is happiest when Max is outside, wonders why I just don't make the sun shine and be done with her brother.

I admit there are times when I act like my cats. I don't like it when a door I want open in my life is suddenly slammed shut. It makes me angry and frustrated, and sometimes, like Max, I run to another door to discover I don't like what's on the other side of that one, either. I sulk and torment anyone in the house until someone fixes the problem—which no one can do. Sometimes it's raining outside all the doors, and I need to practice patience and trust.

I waited patiently for the Lord; he turned to me and heard my cry. —Psalm 40:1

PROCRASTINATION

In general, I do not procrastinate. If I need to be somewhere at a given time, I am usually early; if the garbage needs dumping, my husband dumps it on time. But there are certain activities of everyday life that I put off to the last minute—or beyond.

I food shop when we run out of cat food or toilet paper, not when we run out of fresh vegetables. If we have hash for dinner, that means I'm into my emergency food store and I need to check my supply of cat food and toilet paper. I put off an every-aisle shopping trip not because I hate shopping but because I hate writing large checks, no matter how healthy my checkbook may be.

Sometimes I procrastinate at work, choosing to tackle an interesting project over one that really needs to be done first. I need tight deadlines to keep me on time. Long, compassionate deadlines mean I can put a project off for too long and have to scramble like mad at the last minute.

I'm a selective procrastinator, not a chronic one. No one in my house has ever gone hungry because I've put off shopping, and I seldom miss my deadlines at work, but at times I feel the human urge to kick back and say, "Oh, that can wait a little longer. I'll get to it tomorrow."

I will hasten and not delay to obey your commands. —Psalm 119:60

MAPS

I admire my husband for many reasons, one of which is the fact that he never gets lost. He reads maps for the fun of it. Even though our chances of driving through Antarctica are slim, he will sit for an hour studying the topography of that frozen continent. If we ever get seriously turned around on the way south, he's ready.

I, on the other hand, have been known to forget the way home from the supermarket, especially if we've just moved. I can read a map if

I pull over and stop, but I can't refold an open map, so I never pull over and stop. My dead reckoning is better than my husband's—I never get lost twice in the same place, and I can smell a fast-food restaurant two miles before the golden arches appear on the horizon. I give directions by saying, "Turn left after Joe's Diner"; he says, "Turn north 1.5 miles after the junction of Routes 1 and 287."

Between us we eventually reach most destinations; my way just takes longer. So the next time I find him memorizing a road map of Kent, England, I'll thank the Lord for my husband's attention to details and call the travel agent, knowing we won't get lost on the way to Canterbury.

Each man has his own gift from God; one has this gift, another has that.

—1 Corinthians 7:7

MALLS

Our area has first-class shopping malls every two or three miles on the highway, complete with restaurants, rides for the kids, bowling lanes, theaters, and ice rinks. I hate them all. You can't buy any clothing larger than a size four there. I can spend hours wandering a mall here and never find what I need. It's easier to go downtown and not find what I need.

Yet when we're on vacation I love malls. They fill up a rainy day and give some indication of the spirit of the area, what the people there care about and need in their lives. I especially love malls without a single "designer" store but two or three outdoor supply stores carrying rough woolen jackets, rain gear that keeps you 100 percent dry, and locally made leather shoes.

These malls are small and friendly. They smell of good leather and wet wool, not some French fragrance. The bookstores are full of good mysteries and local lore; the best-seller lists are not displayed by the cash register. The clerks go out of their way to be helpful; the shoppers smile a lot. They are what downtowns used to be before the malls went up on the edges of America. But I bet the residents of that vacation area hate their own malls and can't wait to visit mine. The cement is always grayer on the other side of the fence, you see.

> *But godliness with contentment is great*
> *gain. For we brought nothing into the*
> *world, and we can take nothing out of it.*
> —1 Timothy 6:6–7

WRINKLES

Some cosmetic company sent me a sample container of antiwrinkle face cream to try out, claiming I would see a difference before the container was empty. They were right but not in the way they anticipated. I tried it for a few days, then gave my face a good look under a strong light. Big mistake. I saw every wrinkle, ding, and flaw I have accumulated in sixty-three years—wrinkles I'd never even suspected were there until the magic cream arrived.

I'm still in shock. I don't know if the cream

helped or not because I'd never noticed my face's destruction before and can't make an intelligent comparison. All I know is that my mother's skin now rules my face.

The funny thing is, I don't really remember my mother's skin as being wrinkled. She had freckles that appeared if she stayed in the sun too long, and she burned easily, being a redhead. I remember her dark, kind eyes and her perpetual smile, and I suppose she had her share of what she would call smile lines, but in my mind's eye she is totally without flaw.

I hope my children's memories of me will overlook my flaws, too. In the meantime, I'll use up my sample. It was free, and it taught me some very nice lessons on the art of aging gracefully.

He has made everything beautiful in its time.   —Ecclesiastes 3:11

THE POOL

The house we bought when the children were young came with a huge backyard lawn that we quickly replaced with a swimming pool—a big, beautiful pool that could hold the whole neighborhood at once and still leave room for swimming. We opened it to the neighborhood with only three rules: no unaccompanied children, no glass in the pool area, and each child had to prove he could swim across the deep end before he was allowed out that far. Swimming dogs were not encouraged, either, but a couple did fall in with some regularity.

Despite the work involved, we would do it again in a minute if our kids were young. Our grandchildren are suggesting that we have a huge lawn at our present house, and they could use a pool, but that's not going to happen. We enjoyed the racket and the company of our neighbors; we always knew where the kids were; everyone brought snacks; we're too old to go through it again. We were fortunate enough to be able to pay for the pool's construction but were more than repaid through the lifelong friendships that blossomed in and around the pool's water.

We have since moved to a smaller house, and I understand the pool is now private, which is understandable but sad, but the neighborhood is still a good place to live and a wonderful place to visit when we need to be reminded of the good old days. The pool was the best investment we ever made.

A man of many companions may come to ruin, but there is a friend who sticks closer than a brother. —Proverbs 18:24

PLAY-OFFS

Nobody could resist our pool that day. The air had a bite to it, but the water was warm, steaming slightly like a huge hot tub. Still, we all wanted to watch the play-offs, too. My husband got out his longest extension cord, a neighbor rolled over a portable TV, and we turned on the game. Due to logistics, the only place to put the TV was on the deck at the shallow end of the pool by the wide steps.

We chased the children to the deep end and sank up to our shoulders in the warm water, looking remarkably like the well-known picture of Japanese monkeys enjoying the warmth of a spring in the middle of a snowstorm. We set out snacks at the pool's edge (normally not allowed that close to the water) and gave the kids their own snacks elsewhere. I think there were about eight adults and eight children in the water that day, some playing, some watching the game and swimming at the same time, others just bobbing around. This was an "adult swim" event, so no games of Marco Polo were allowed (What fool came up with that game?).

On the next weekend, the pool would be covered and closed for the winter, and the next football game would be watched from our homes, but for that day we had it all—good friends, warm water, and football—all at once!

> . . . *God, who richly provides us with*
> *everything for our enjoyment.*
>
> —1 Timothy 6:17

BOREDOM

Between losing a job, finding another, and shoulder surgery, my husband has been home for two months. He's so bored that his face falls if I bring in the morning paper and rob him of two minutes of productivity. He's learning to play Free Cell on the computer; he loaded a music program so he can listen to low-fidelity music while he stares at the monitor. He watches fishing programs for two hours a day, afraid that's all the fishing he will be able to enjoy this season.

Some men might relish a two-month holiday, but this one has to be busy to be happy, and it's hard to be busy when you can't move one arm. So he paces. For hours on end he walks from room to room, picking up little specks of dust and stray cat-food pellets, sitting down only when it's time to put an ice pack on his shoulder. When he gets bored with pacing, he goes out and picks up sticks in the yard that he would normally have in peak condition by now.

In two days the stitches come out, and he gets to move his arm; a week after that he goes back to work. I hope. It's hard not to feel sorry for a caged animal, especially if you're married to him.

> *I will tell of the kindnesses of the Lord, the deeds for which he is to be praised, according to all the Lord has done for us—yes, the many good things he has done. . . according to his compassion and many kindnesses.* —Isaiah 63:7

BEAR

It took years of vacationing in the woods before I saw my first bear in the wild. I'd seen the south end of a northbound bear as he dove into the bushes, but that didn't count. I'd seen bear tracks and bear scat and once caught the smell of a bear—unpleasant, to say the least—but never got a real look at one until an abnormal black smudge under a tree caught my attention. My guide slowed the truck to a crawl, and there the bear was, taking a nap in the shade on a hot summer day.

"Three hundred. . .three-fifty pounds," the guide estimated. The bear lifted his head and searched for our scent, didn't like what he smelled, and stood up. "He'll run," the guide predicted.

I was torn by two opposing desires. I could reach for my camera or keep my eyes on the bear and forget the picture. I voted for watching. So big, so powerful—there would be no getting out of the truck for a better view of this animal! The bear, still groggy from the sun, slowly turned and walked off into the woods, dismissing us as nothing to be concerned about. In less than a minute he'd been there and then was gone.

"You didn't get a picture?" the guide asked.

I pointed to my head. "I got him here. That's enough."

The blessing of the Lord brings wealth,
and he adds no trouble to it.

—Proverbs 10:22

MORE BEAR

Again we were driving the logging roads in search of wildlife, taking a break from fishing on a windy day. We were inching along a particularly rough road with washouts on both sides when three dark bodies streaked across the road in front of us—a mother bear and roly-poly twins.

Mama wanted the twins to put plenty of distance between themselves and our stopped truck, but one of them bounded up a tree for a better look. Many times that had been the appropriate reaction to danger, but this time the order was to run. Even when she growled at him, he stayed in the tree, peeking through the branches at us. He was all fur and big, curious eyes—lovable as he could be with a mother that ugly. Mama sent her one obedient child off into the woods with a snarl, hesitated a second in indecision, then climbed the tree and knocked the disobedient one to the ground with a great swat. He tumbled down noisily, head over heels, squealing at the injustice of his punishment, and followed her off reluctantly.

I hoped that cub had learned his lesson, because his disobedience could have cost all three of them their lives in different circumstances. His mother had risked everything to save him from what she thought was immediate danger. Apparently child rearing can even be difficult for bears.

Train a child in the way he should go, and when he is old he will not turn from it.
—Proverbs 22:6

BAD DREAM

I have a recurring dream in which my faithful husband walks off with a younger woman, leaving me with nothing—no home, no cash, no father for the children I can no longer support. I wake up angry—no, furious—sometimes even punching him in my sleep and yelling, "How dare you?"

He, of course, is rightfully indignant. "What did you dream I did now?" he will ask, hiding under the blankets.

"You. . .you. . .you *know!*"

Now my adrenaline is really pumping, and I'm just plain mad at him. He may not have left me, but there's other ammunition I could use if I wanted to. Fortunately I've learned to shut up and calm down before I say something stupid and provoke a battle based on an irrational dream that was caused by pizza in the first place. It still bugs me a little that he never shows any guilt at all, though. He was a real rotter in that dream!

> *Starting a quarrel is like breaching a dam;*
> *so drop the matter before a dispute breaks*
> *out.*   —Proverbs 17:14

ON TIME

I'm not very time sensitive. Most of my life is ruled by what needs to be done, not by the time of day. I can afford this luxury because I'm self-employed, the kids are grown, and my husband knows the time to the second. He will be napping on the couch in the evening and suddenly snap wide awake to tell me it's time to go to sleep. If he says we will be somewhere at 2:15, we will arrive between 2:13 and 2:17. At times he has been known to park around the block and wait until the appointed time to pull into our hosts' driveway. People have bet against us and lost.

While his time sensitivity gets us places on time, my lack of it gets us there in good moods. Well, it gets *me* there in a good mood, anyway. He may still be fuming about the traffic tie-up that threw his schedule off by ten minutes.

The differences between us could be a recipe for marital disaster. Instead we find that our differences actually work for us, not against us. Calculating his arrival time keeps him awake on a long drive, leaving me free to see and share interesting sights along the way. Our differences in viewpoint make us both more complete individuals and a unit of one where once we were just two people going off in different directions and getting there at two different times.

Two are better than one, because they have
a good return for their work: If one falls
down, his friend can help him up.
—Ecclesiastes 4:9–10

HORROR STORIES

Now that our children are full grown, they're beginning to fill us in on their childhood, that time of life when we thought our vigilance alone kept them alive. We always knew where they were and who they were with— or so we thought until two of them laughed about exploring the neighborhood storm drain system and traveling the pipes to sneak up on the children from the next block. Thoughts of rats and filth and sudden downpours filled me with horror. The kids laughed at me, then went on to tell the tale of the neighborhood boy who had barely been talked down from a roof before he tried to disprove the law of gravity. The stories went on and on, and my vision of being a good mother for all those years began to fade. Still, they somehow all survived and grew into perfectly normal adults—a blessing we no longer attribute to our own efforts.

No matter how vigilant parents are, they cannot possibly be everywhere, see everything, and have all the answers. Even the best of kids must try the patience of their guardian angels in their explorations of life. With the emergence of every horrifying tale our children now feel free to tell us, God's protection and love become even more real and miraculous to us. We had done a decent job but not on our own, and we gave thanks for all those busy, patient angels that hung around for so many years.

But let all who take refuge in you be glad; let them ever sing for joy. Spread your protection over them, that those who love your name may rejoice in you. —Psalm 5:11

MARRIAGE STYLES

My husband and I both work on the simple premise that if you really like someone or something you'd better not say so, or someone will tax it, maim it, or take it away from you. It's not easy being this cynical, believe me, but we have no desire to speak to a professional about it, because we have worked out a happy marriage around a mutually warped viewpoint. I'm sure there are others doing equally well under worse psychological burdens.

Besides, it keeps us on our toes. Not being

mawkishly demonstrative, we have to find other ways to show our affection. We boast about each other, though never when the other can hear—although we usually do hear. We don't buy roses or greeting cards but look for genuine little wants and present them without fanfare on a Tuesday (the worst day of any week). I cook his favorite meal on a day when I would prefer take-out, and he takes me fishing when he would really rather go alone. I tell him I like his bald spot, and he tells me he likes women with meat on their bones (both are not true, but who cares?).

Who's to say what makes a good marriage? Sometimes God graces the most unusual relationships, the ones everyone else believes are doomed to fail. As some wise person once said, "Whatever floats your boat."

> *"Never will I leave you; never will I forsake you."* —Hebrews 13:5

YORKSHIRE
AND KENT

When we took a family trip to England, we stayed one week with a farm family in North Yorkshire and another week on a farm in Kent. The two areas are only a nice train ride apart. Both sets of hosts were genuinely friendly and kind, eager to talk with us and tell us about special places to visit. They fed us like kings, and our children played together happily. Despite their very different ways of speaking English, they were very much alike.

Seeing us off, the Yorkshire couple leaned into the car to warn us that the people in Kent are very different—cold, not friendly like those in Yorkshire. They thought we should know this. When we arrived in Kent, our hosts there told us people from Yorkshire are very different—cold, not friendly like those in Kent. I wanted to give them each other's address and suggest they visit on their next holiday. Both couples agreed that people from London were cold, not friendly, so they might get along very well.

I suppose it's the same everywhere, no matter what country you visit, and only outsiders can see the truth that most people are naturally friendly and kind, no matter where they live. Now when I find myself thinking about those (choose your group), I remember our trip and our two sets of hosts, wonderful people all, worthy of God's love and mine, not to mention each other's.

You are no longer foreigners and aliens,
but fellow citizens with God's people and
members of God's household.

—Ephesians 2:19

MOOSE

I know that God has a sense of humor. He did, after all, create the moose, which looks like a horse gone incredibly wrong. I met my first moose in the middle of an isolated logging road. We made the mistake of rounding a blind bend a little too fast, coming face-to-knee with a young animal who stood his ground in true moose fashion. My first thought was, *He's so big!* Television or photographs do not convey the sheer massiveness of a moose—even a young one.

Moose are not overly intelligent. Fortunately,

they are exceedingly calm, collected animals, curious and patient with humans who invade their space. They look us over and usually decide we're no threat—not a wise decision during hunting season. This particular moose blocked the road for a good ten minutes to look us over before ambling off into the bushes on moose business.

No human who has ever shared space with a moose can avoid loving them. Their ugliness, their bony long legs, their cowlike eyes—you just can't resist them, even though you know they can do fatal damage if they collide with a car. They are somewhat like an ugly baby—always a surprise, but one that makes you smile in spite of yourself and thank God for providing such unexpected delight. God didn't make the moose beautiful or smart, just irresistible, and seeing a moose can only be considered a blessing.

God made the wild animals according to
their kinds, the livestock. . .and all the
creatures that move along the ground
according to their kinds. And God saw
that it was good.   —Genesis 1:25

BASS

My cousin and I used to fish every evening after dinner when I visited their camp. The rule was that the first kids to get the fishing rods down off the nails in the beam got to fish. The fix was in, since my cousin towered over her brothers. My job was to block the two boys while she snagged the rods.

It never really dawned on us that sometime we might actually catch a fish. There were bass in the lake, but none of them ever bothered us. We'd just float and cast until darkness fell and my aunt lit the kerosene lamps to guide us home.

But one night one of us (I don't recall which) actually hooked a bass and pulled it into the rowboat, where it flapped away, scaring us both to death. We did what any kid would do: We yelled for my poor uncle, who raced to the dock convinced we had tipped over. "What's the matter?" he yelled.

"We can't get the fish off the hook!" we yelled back.

"Hit it on the head and bring it in. Do you expect me to walk on water?"

Well, actually we hoped he would. We brought the fish in alive, my cousin rowing like mad and me keeping one eye on the fish and another on the safety of the dock. My uncle insisted we kill the fish and clean it ourselves; my aunt cooked it for breakfast the next day. It was the best breakfast of my life.

You made him ruler over the works of your hands. . .the birds of the air, and the fish of the sea.

—Psalm 8:6, 8

NORTHERN DAWN

I woke up fuzzy and disoriented until I heard the muffled thunk of the cruise ship's engines. It was light enough that I could clearly see my watch's face: 3:00 A.M.! Dawn was breaking, and I was wide awake, a victim of jet lag after a fourteen-hour flight to Alaska. I threw on a warm jacket and jeans and left my husband, who never gets jet lag, sleeping peacefully. Two short lefts and I was on the bow of the promenade deck, huddled up against what I would call a wall (bulkhead?).

When a brand-new shaft of warm sunlight hit my face, I looked up and gasped. Spread before me was an Alaskan fjord. We floated on strange blue-green, semiopaque water; glaciers sparkled on the sides of the mountains that climbed straight out of the sea and up to the bottom of the clouds. Two quick rights and I was back in our cabin, shaking my husband. "Get up! You've got to see this!" A short while later there were about fifteen of us shivering and yawning on deck, whispering among ourselves, not wanting to wake up anyone else. This was our dawn—our beauty—we didn't need more company. A window opened above us, and a face looked down from the bridge. "Good morning, East Coasters. Coffee and Danish are in the lounge if you need them. Isn't it worth the fourteen-hour plane ride?"

Oh yes, it certainly was!

"Your eyes will see the king in his beauty
and view a land that stretches afar."

—Isaiah 33:17

WARM SPRINGS BAY

Our small cruise ship made a slow turn and headed out of the channel toward the forested shoreline just as the sun began to set. Where were we headed? Our itinerary said Warm Springs Bay, Baranof Island, Alaska, but we saw no bay ahead, just ranks of fir-covered mountains. Another slight direction change and the tiny bay was suddenly off our bow. A sixty-foot waterfall poured into it dead ahead with a roar; a collection of little buildings clung to the limited space between bay and mountain; fishing boats rocked gently. Above all stood the mountains that protected the bay and cut it off from civilization at the same time.

We normally raucous passengers grew silent while the captain guided us to our night's anchorage in the middle of the bay, threading the needle carefully because of the limited space he had for maneuvering. Gulls flew overhead in welcome. People on the shore waved and went about their business; fishermen began heading out for a night's work. Cameras clicked and whirred, but the bay was so small that two shots got it all, and silence returned.

The next day we would explore the area, stopping to wash our hands in the warm water that ran freely down the edges of the trail we would hike to a mountain pond. We would learn how the people living there heated their homes with the warm springs and generated their own electricity with the waterfall, but nothing would surpass our entry into this little paradise at sunset.

Praise the Lord from the heavens, praise
him in the heights above. Praise him, all

his angels, praise him, all his heavenly
hosts. . .for he commanded and they were
created. —Psalm 148:1–2, 5

LOST KING

We are catch-and-release fishermen, but you don't throw back a fifty-pound king salmon in Alaska. Your lodge has it processed, flash frozen, and transported to the airport in a cooler for loading onto your flight. It is taken for granted that this is what you want. From the time you pull the fish onto the dock until you reach the luggage pick-up at your airport, you never see the package. That does not mean you and your salmon will arrive home the same day, however. You can run to catch a connecting flight, but the salmon can't, which is why we spent our first three days at home on the telephone with three airlines, the lodge owner, and the fish packer. We were home, but our fish was still somewhere between Alaska and the East Coast—and it was thawing!

The lodge owner said it would be frozen solid for three to four days, and when it finally was delivered to our home only the top layer was showing signs of beginning to defrost. We disbursed that layer to friends and coworkers immediately (warning them to cook it that night) and enjoyed the remainder on the grill with lemon and dill for the rest of the summer.

Looking back on it, it was sort of funny. The fish that we so reluctantly accepted and allowed to be shipped home wasn't that important to us until it got lost. Only then, when defrosting seemed certain, did we root for our fish to make it home safely.

" 'Rejoice with me; I have found my lost sheep.' "
—Luke 15:6

TRUST

My husband is about as trustworthy as anyone I know. If necessary he would throw himself in front of a bullet for me. If that failed, I could die knowing he would be able to give a detailed, accurate description of my attacker that would bring him to justice.

So why don't I trust him to stay awake on a long drive? True, he did fall asleep once in thirty-eight years, but not recently. My distrust has turned on me, too. Now that he knows I'll watch him for signs of sleepiness, keeping him alert has become my job, not his. I'm the one who has to decide if we stop for coffee now or thirty miles later. I'm the one who has to offer to drive (something neither of us wants). It's my responsibility to be so aggravating that neither of us can enjoy the scenery, because when he's enjoying himself he is often asleep.

On the other hand, he will never trust me to hang a picture or operate garden machinery. I'm not precise enough for hanging pictures. I don't carefully measure and center the nail on the wall, allowing for the drop in the back. My picture arrangements are decidedly informal. As far as garden machinery goes, I tend to get irrational when a piece of mechanized iron refuses to obey me, and no sane man would let me anywhere near a weed whip. I am allowed to watch him mow the lawn, though—just in case he falls asleep.

Cast all your anxiety on him because he
cares for you. —1 Peter 5:7

"WAIT UNTIL. . ."

The most-hated words in our family when the children were young were "Wait until your father comes home!" They hated it; my husband really hated it. Well, I still say that phrase has its place and purpose.

First, it kept the offender alive for a few more hours. By the time I was driven to say those words, I was beyond reason and needed to back off. We all needed a time-out. Second, they knew without a doubt that the precipitating misbehavior was serious—very serious. I probably only said it two or three times to each child. Third, they were his kids, too, and he should be the bad guy once in awhile.

Most of the time he did exactly what I would have done if I could speak at all—he grounded them for a little less than life (that's two weeks in teenage time). They accepted his judgment knowing they would have fared worse at my hands. Once it was over, we got on with our lives with few hard feelings.

Even now that phrase is hanging around in my life, not in reference to the children, but in reference to me. Sometimes I behave poorly. I lose my temper at small, silly things; I do something that will cause another pain; I don't engage brain before speaking. A split second before I lash out, my guardian angel will whisper in my ear: "Wait until *your* Father comes home!" It still works.

Endure hardship as discipline; God is treating you as sons. For what son is not disciplined by his father?

—Hebrews 12:7

BEN

My children would not forgive me if I didn't mention Ben. Ben was the dog of their childhood. He was named for a pastor we once knew and grew to deserve his name, which to us represented faithfulness, compassion, and a willingness to go the extra mile for those he served. Ben was the perfect dog, totally without doggy flaw. A toddler could pull his ears without fear; a kitten could use him as a pillow and pull toy. He might bark at a stranger but would lick a burglar to death.

Ben was not a wimp, however. He positioned himself between our children and strangers, all the time politely wagging his tail. He feared thunder, but when it made him cower under a bed, it was always a bed with a child in it. If guardian angels ever take earthly form, Ben qualified for the job.

Ben was also a bird dog. He helped teach our sons how to hunt pheasant, no matter how sharp the thorns or how hot the day. He would drown before failing to retrieve a bird lying at the water's edge. There have been other dogs in our lives, but there was only one Ben.

As I think of him, I do remember his one doggy flaw. Like all dogs, he loved drinking out of the toilet. Other than that, he was the perfect dog.

" 'Well done, good and faithful servant! . . .
Come and share your master's happiness!' "
—Matthew 25:21

TINA

Tina was the second dog of our marriage, the first female. She pretended to love me because her real master, my husband, did. She didn't fool me; I saw through her deception. All day she would follow me around the house to be sure I didn't damage anything. When she slept, she always turned her back on me. Mostly, she ignored me.

When her master appeared, she was a model dog, showering him with affection and attention. He thought it was cute when she curled up between us on the couch; he was pleased that she ate only food prepared by his hands. She had him wrapped around her paw.

For the sake of my husband and the children, Tina and I pretended to get along just fine. In time we even developed a warped affection for each other, but the truth was that she saw herself as the alpha female of the family, not me. I didn't much like that.

As we both aged, I was allowed to pet her at will and even feed her. She decided I was worth protecting from squirrels and unknown dogs. My husband was allowed to hug me. Time reduced the jealousy between us, and when we made the final trip to the vet's, I was allowed to hold her in my arms. She was a good dog.

Anger is cruel and fury overwhelming, but who can stand before jealousy?
—Proverbs 27:4

GRANKEE AND BEEBOP

When our grandson more or less learned to talk, he went through his "Adam phase," where he named everything in his universe. Somehow I became Grankee; my husband was Beebop. Grankee I could understand as a combined form of "Grandma" and "Toni." Someone said he was really trying to say "Cranky," but he didn't have a mean bone in his body, so I accepted the name of Grankee in good faith. But what did Beebop stand for? Certainly not any music he had heard at our house. Then one day he came for a visit while my husband was at work, looked around expectantly, and asked, "Beebop?"

"Grandpa's at work," I explained. Although his speech was a little erratic, he understood anything you said to him, so I talked to him as if he were an adult and explained anything that might confuse him.

His face fell. "Beebop?" We checked every room in the house, his disappointment growing by the minute.

"He's not here, Nick. I'm sorry. He'll be back soon."

"Beebop," Nick stated with authority, a smile on his face. Something had comforted him, but I didn't know what.

And the light went on. Beebop was both a name *and* a verb. Grandpa would be back soon—Beebop: "be back," in Nick's language.

It didn't take Nick very long to learn to say Grandma and Grandpa, but for a precious few months we were joyously happy to be Grankee and Beebop.

*He brought them to the man to see what
he would name them; and whatever the
man called each living creature, that was
its name.* —Genesis 2:19

TYRANNY

For thirty-eight years I have ruled the clicker of our television set through default. My husband will fall asleep no matter what's on and doesn't really care what he sleeps through, so the job is mine. At first I tried to involve him, asking if he preferred to watch this or that. His answer was always "Whatever you want." A good answer; a wise answer!

Occasionally he'll awake, pick up a magazine to indicate his displeasure with my choice, read a page or two, then fall asleep with the magazine in his lap. If I choose a noisy show, he may actually watch it for a few minutes before nodding off, but sleep is inevitable.

But he's getting assertive in his old age. He has one or two shows he actually enjoys—shows I don't enjoy myself but watch to please him. I try to be a benevolent despot of the clicker. Once in awhile he will actually pick up the clicker and surf the channels, something guaranteed to get my back up. That's not his job, and I retake possession of the clicker as soon as he puts it down, sometimes silently placing it far out of his reach. We don't argue about this—it's *my* clicker, after all, no poaching allowed.

This is what marriage is all about: coming to agreement one way or another, respecting the other's wishes, and trusting one or the other to possession of the clicker.

Be of one mind, live in peace. And the God of love and peace will be with you.
— 2 Corinthians 13:11

SOCIAL SECURITY

The day my first Social Security check arrived was a red-letter day. Free money—from the government, yet! Oh, I'd known I qualified. I'd filled out all the forms; I'd taken in all the proofs required; I'd even clarified points on the telephone, but that was months ago, and frankly I was sure something would go wrong, so I didn't count any chickens until the deposit appeared on my bank statement. Even then, I restrained my wonder. Something could still go wrong. The cynic in me was not ready to admit that things could also go right from time to time, even when the government was involved.

The real surprise was when the second check arrived right on time, then the third. My checkbook's balance was slowly growing with no effort at all on my part. The checks will keep coming, too (or so they say), as long as I'm around to bank them. I couldn't live on them, but they do provide a nice little cushion for emergencies.

My husband laughs at my surprise every month and the little dance I do when the bank statement arrives and proves the system is still paying me to breathe, but he's never been poor. He's rarely had a bank account that leaks money like a sieve. To him it's just a bureaucratic process; to me it's a wonder. Free money!

And God is able to make all grace abound
to you, so that in all things at all times,
having all that you need, you will abound
in every good work.

—2 Corinthians 9:8

THE PERCH

Our cats share a perch in front of the kitchen windows overlooking the backyard. It has a scratching post and two sitting platforms covered with rug remnants. One of the cats is always sitting on the top perch, sleeping on it in the sun, or trying to evict the current occupant (the lower perch is in some way inferior). Sometimes they are so overcome by contentment that they stretch out and sleep too soundly, falling to the floor in a furry thud.

The cats spend hours guarding the backyard

from tiny birds and squirrels, chattering their teeth in fury anytime some creature touches the back deck. Most of the time their stare is fixed on something we can't even see. Their rapt attention stops us in our tracks and makes us follow their gazes until we see the nuthatch working on the suet feeder or the butterfly dancing through the perennial bed.

We love the perch because it helps us see all the little things going on outside that we would otherwise miss. It encourages us to get a cup of coffee and relax. We don't have time for that, but when the cats are on point we know something unusual is going on, something the cats believe we really should take notice of. The cats are usually quite correct: We need a break, and from the perch they will protect the backyard while we enjoy the view.

> *I have learned the secret of being content in any and every situation, whether well fed or hungry, whether living in plenty or in want.* —Philippians 4:12

THE GIFT

I grew up in a college town. My parents had professors as friends, and I played with their children, but when it was time to apply to college I never gave it a thought. I was prepared to go into the service and get an education there. But one day a professor we knew handed me a college application to fill out, although he knew we couldn't pay the tuition. A few weeks later it was all worked out: We would pay what we could (next to nothing), I would work on campus when I could, and the rest of the cost would just go away.

Even at eighteen, I knew this was remarkable. This wasn't some little state college; it was a well-respected, expensive institution. I couldn't afford any college, let alone this one. Well, I was no fool—I took the gift and ran with it. I felt I had a duty to do well, so I worked hard and did decently. Looking back, I can see that the opportunity given to me was part good will and part good public relations on the part of the college. To me, it was all a blessing, a gift, a chance to get ahead. Financially I have more than repaid the college, but in my heart I will never be able to repay anyone involved. Having this kind of debt is just one sign of an abundant life.

"I know your deeds, your love and faith, your service and perseverance."
—Revelation 2:19

THE SINK

All my grandchildren ask of me is that I have some snacks and soda in the house and let them play in the kitchen sink. They can spend hours up to their elbows in soapy water floating boats or having a soapsuds battle. I try to leave them some dirty dishes to wash, rinse, and dry. If they do a good job, they get to dip into the change jar on the counter. (I turned down my granddaughter's offer to do the dishes for seven dollars; she settled for pennies.)

I don't understand their motivation. It's true

that their mother doesn't let them play in her sink—it's just another mess for her to clean up— but they get away with plenty at home. For some reason, going to Grandma's has to involve water in a sink, even if I relieve them of their soaking wet shirts and toss them into the drier when they're done.

We have plenty of games, two TV sets, paper and pens, and a computer with games, but it's the sink they want. Do they remember me giving them baths there when they were young and slippery? Is it the deepness of the sink that makes it attractive? I don't know, but I do know that when I'm gone they'll remember me as the one who let them get soaking wet in the kitchen sink. And that's okay by me.

"You will be like a well-watered garden,
like a spring whose waters never fail."

—Isaiah 58:11

"WHAT?"

My ears are not what they used to be. Neither are my husband's, so our conversations often go, "Mumble, mumble?"

"Huh?"

"Mumble!"

"Well, you don't have to yell!"

It's gotten bad enough that I have been known to watch television shows in Spanish until he walks in and asks, "Mumble Spanish?"

"Is this in Spanish?"

"Huh?"

Australian and other English dialects are beyond me. I can only catch phrases here and there, which pretty much rules out BBC shows. I'm aging from the top down. My eyes have always been bad; now my ears are failing. What's next, my nose? I don't know how noses fail as they age, but it can't be pleasant.

And people think getting old is boring. Not with all the involuntary changes going on around here. Not only are our muscles failing, now it's our passive receptors. Are there exercises we can do to fix our hearing or sight? Would carrots help? Or worse yet, okra? If we really work at it—lift some weights or take up jogging—is that going to stop our creeping sensory deprivation? No, self-improvement has its limits. I think the only thing to do is accept our aging as it comes and learn to laugh at life's little challenges.

Do not cast me away when I am old; do
not forsake me when my strength is gone.

—Psalm 71:9

F O G

The float plane coming in to take us to another lake for a day's fishing was late, the reason obvious. Standing on the shore, we could not see the end of the dock through the fog. The pilot would be lucky to find the lake, let alone a break in the fog to risk an attempt at landing. Soon we could hear him circling above us, around and around, searching for the one small, clear spot he needed to find his way down. A few more attempts and he would be forced to give up and return to his base, short of fuel. The sound of the engine changed, and suddenly there he was, skiing up to the dock as if a magician had waved a magic wand.

"Come on; come on!" the pilot yelled out his open window. We grabbed our gear and ran down the dock. Minutes later we were buckled in and on our way down the lake at full speed. But what were we speeding toward? "No problem," the pilot yelled to me—a notoriously poor flyer—over the roar of the engine. "See that spot of sun? That's all we need." Sure enough, I saw one tiny break in the fog. We flew toward the light, fog all around us, then broke through into a bright, clear fall day.

Below us, the whole lake was again covered in fog. Even our little light spot was gone, but we were safe. It looked like a good day for fishing.

"I am the light of the world. Whoever follows me will never walk in darkness, but will have the light of life." —John 8:12

COOKING

After thirty-eight years of marriage, I am sick of cooking. I did the balanced-meal routine as long as there was a child in the house—guilt is a great motivator—but now that it's just the two of us at the dinner table, I'm getting lax. Sometimes I don't bother with a vegetable, figuring I'll make up for it the next day with two vegetables and no potato. Most of the time the next day will feature pizza (tomato sauce must count as a vegetable).

My husband does not seem to be wasting

away, and I'm certainly not. Once or twice a week I go hog-wild and make a pot roast or chicken stew or a meal in the Crock-Pot (that virtually cooks itself). I love old-fashioned food but not as much as I hate the cooking itself. Generally, if a meal can't get to the table in fifteen to twenty minutes, it's not going to be on the menu.

My husband seems to understand, unless I send him for take-out more than two days a week. From what I hear, a lot of women are sick of cooking or never learned how to cook; I'm hardly in the minority. So why do I feel so guilty?

A man can do nothing better than to eat and drink and find satisfaction in his work. This too, I see, is from the hand of God, for without him, who can eat or find enjoyment? —Ecclesiastes 2:24–25

SIMPLE FAITH

It's extremely difficult for us to live in faith, because doing so means giving up on our own efforts, and we are a nation of doers. If asked, most of us would say we have faith, that we believe God cares for us and will always give us His best. But we worry about the details a lot. God will provide for us one way or another, but will we like the way it all works out? Can we help? Can our science and technology change the timetable a little? How much meddling can we engage in and still say we have faith?

I don't personally think God expects us to sit back and wait for Him. He gives us knowledge for a reason, so why not make good use of it? If we goof up, do we really not believe God is capable of correcting our errors and showing us a better way?

And yet we know there is much that requires faith, so much we cannot do ourselves. Here is where we meet simple faith. We do the best we can as earthly creatures; the rest we must leave to God in faith. Sometimes faith is dynamic and purposeful; other times it is simply waiting and trusting. The truth is, waiting and trusting are harder than doing. They require more of us and teach us patience in the face of adversity.

> *Let us draw near to God with a sincere heart in full assurance of faith. . . . Let us hold unswervingly to the hope we profess, for he who promised is faithful.*
>
> —Hebrews 10:22–23

JUNK CALLS

I recently learned how to spot a telephone salesperson before he or she says a word. I say "Hello," count to two, and hang up in that split second of airy silence before they come on the line and begin the pitch. Anything automated can be foiled if you see the pattern. If my reaction time is a little slow, the salesperson only has two seconds to mispronounce my name before I hang up.

My husband loves to play mind games with the salesperson. He will listen to the whole pitch, no matter how long it may be, then demolish the caller's logic point by point, demonstrating how the deal we have now is far better than what they are offering. I can imagine them quivering like gelatin as the conversation goes way beyond their script.

What upsets me about these calls is that they have changed us for the worse. I am not the type of person who hangs up on others. My husband is not a cruel person who belittles or intimidates others. I fear that someday I will hang up on someone I know. I suppose these calls do sell something—they wouldn't use them if they didn't—but they are making us all a little more rude, a little less considerate, and a whole lot angrier than we really need to be.

Be kind and compassionate to one another,
forgiving each other, just as in Christ God
forgave you. —Ephesians 4:32

SWEET DEAL

People who find out what I do for a living think I have a sweet deal. "You read and write books? You get paid to read?" Well, yes, I do, although not all that well. I don't get to choose what I read, and my eyesight is getting worse every year, thanks to small print and computer glare, but it could be said I get paid to read.

Frankly, it's about the only thing I do reasonably well. I was always on the losing side of office politics, so it's a good thing I don't have an office. Writing is a solitary profession, which suits me fine, but it's not that easy. On a bad day I may work ridiculously hard just to complete one type-written page, go back and edit it, then end up throwing it away and checking out the want ads for another job—any other job. Ideas are hard to come by; deadlines are often impossibly close. Glamorous it isn't, but it's my job.

I don't know why God gave me this job. I sort of like the idea of being a stone mason, but that must be awfully hard on the hands. I'd like to be a professional fisherman, but I don't really like boats. Somehow God took account of all my abilities, preferences, and characteristics and decided I could best be of service if left alone to read and write for a living. It really *is* a sweet deal!

We are the clay, you are the potter; we are
all the work of your hand.

—Isaiah 64:8

PRAYER

Some people find it difficult to pray, even when they have an immediate need and suspect that the help they desire can only come from God. They don't want to bother God; He has to be busy. Then there's the Santa Claus problem: You don't want to make the list too long, or you may not get what you really want. Others just feel unworthy—who are they to ask for help when the world is full of more deserving people? All these worries are perfectly human, but they all do injustice to God.

God *wants* us to talk to Him, to ask for His help, and believe He will give it in love. He's not too busy, and the number of prayers He will consider has no limit. Our requests are considered individually, not put on some heavenly "to do" list ranked according to seriousness or worthiness. When we pray, we have God's complete attention. When He answers, He does so in perfect love, even when the answer is "not now."

There are no rules about praying. We can pray in church or driving on the interstate. No fancy words are necessary because God knows what we need before we even ask. We may pray in misery or joy, for large problems or small, silently or out loud. God just wants to hear from us now and then, like a parent with grown children welcomes an unexpected phone call. Keep in touch.

Be joyful always; pray continually; give thanks in all circumstances, for this is God's will for you in Christ Jesus.

—1 Thessalonians 5:16–18

WORK

Work has been with us since the beginning of time. God worked out creation before He rested. Adam and Eve were the stewards of Eden before they caused their own demotion to hard physical labor. The apostles were responsible for bringing salvation to the whole world. With examples such as these, it's obvious that work has value in God's sight.

Granted, few of us are entrusted with earth-shaking positions, and none of our examples had to put up with our bosses (although Paul was certainly a demanding supervisor), but we are all capable of honest toil in the home, office, or shop. Whatever we do can be done to the glory of God. Whatever we learn can serve as an example for others. No work lacks value, and all work is a blessing.

Work gives us part of our human identity. When we introduce ourselves to others we first give them our name, then mention what we "do." Of course we're much more than a name and occupation, but this suffices for a casual introduction. Our work, whatever it may be, says we are a productive person, one who is contributing to the common welfare and is therefore a person of value. No matter what we work at, our efforts can bring glory to God, which is work's highest ideal.

May the favor of the Lord our God rest upon us; establish the work of our hands for us—yes, establish the work of our hands. —Psalm 90:17

STORM

The storm came out of the west when we were gathering by the resort's lodge waiting for the dinner bell. The sky to the west darkened as though a light had suddenly been turned off. We saw a wall of water approaching faster than seemed possible, heard its trainlike roar as it was blown toward us in the form of horizontal rain. Fortunately, fishermen being reliably hungry people, no one was out on the lake.

Guides raced to secure boats to the lee side of the dock. Children playing by the water were called onto the porch. The camp dog, smarter than the rest of us, coiled herself under a sturdy bench that was nailed to a wall and waited.

Soon it was impossible to stay on the porch, so we filed inside and crowded the windows, watching life preservers being flung like leaves and boats straining at their ropes. How could such a small lake produce such huge whitecaps? In five minutes, it was over. The sun came back out; we gathered up the life preservers; the dog reappeared. We hung up our soaked jackets and went in to dinner considerably more reverent toward nature's unexpected fury than we had ever been before. But everyone was accounted for, and fishing would be great after the storm.

A furious squall came up, and the waves broke over the boat. . . . He said to his disciples, "Why are you so afraid? Do you still have no faith?" —Mark 4:37, 40

SIBLINGS

I always wanted a brother or sister while I was growing up, but it didn't happen. My friends would constantly complain about their brothers and sisters, and I would feel sorry for them because they didn't know a good thing when they lived with it. With two working parents, I knew all too well the silence of an empty house.

Looking back on it, being an only child was not that bad. If I needed a houseful of children, I would go visit a friend and come home welcoming the peace and quiet. I learned to talk to adults at an early age. I discovered the companionship of books. I learned to be alone but not feel lonely. When I got to the age when other children were really necessary, I played after-school sports. I learned to cope, in other words.

Still, even now I sometimes wish I had a sister I could call on a rainy day, a blood relative who would know me and know exactly what I need to hear. Now that my earthly family is getting smaller as age takes its toll, I find myself turning to my constant friend, my brother Jesus, who always knows what's bothering me and what I need to hear. I suspect that's why I never really felt lonely as an only child.

"Here are my mother and my brothers. For whoever does the will of my Father in heaven is my brother and sister and mother." —Matthew 12:49–50

CANTERBURY

I found my great-grandparents' graves in Canterbury cemetery. The plot was in bad shape but not gruesome, and their names and dates were still readable on the plain stone that listed quite a bit to the left. I had found my roots, one of the reasons we had brought the three kids, ages eight, eleven, and fourteen, with us.

We were spending three weeks in the United Kingdom, staying on farms and trying to remember that "left is right" when it comes to driving there. The kids rapidly "castled-out," sick of historic sites that meant nothing to them and dying for an edible pizza, but now things had somehow changed.

"Can you stand one more old church?" I asked, waiting for their groans. This was a rhetorical question; no way were they not going to Canterbury Cathedral!

"Did your great-grandparents go to church there?" one of them asked.

"I imagine they did, although they were Methodists, so maybe not."

"But they saw it, didn't they? Every day."

"Yes, every day. It was part of their lives, no matter where they went to church."

"Yeah. I want to see it, too."

We left the cemetery no longer having to drag our children through historic sites. This was family history, far more important than regular old stones. Those stones were our stones now, and we all needed to see them.

Whatever is has already been, and what will be has been before; and God will call the past to account. —Ecclesiastes 3:15

CRAFTSMEN

We have been blessed in finding good craftsmen. We found a car mechanic whose work is impeccable, who would never even dream of ripping us off. Our plumber will drop everything and appear the day we need him. He knows all the other craftsmen in the area and diplomatically steers us away from those he doesn't trust. If he doesn't know one we have engaged, he will come to check out his work. If the contractor doesn't like it, too bad.

Our appliance saleswoman is a craftsman, too.

We found a lack of functioning appliances in our new house—what we needed was either missing or not working, not to mention antique. In a hectic, rather frightening two hours we ordered what we needed, arranged for prompt delivery, and got our store line of credit extended—no forms, no signatures, no waiting.

Our roofer left three nails in the driveway; three out of the hundreds he took off the old roof. Everything that came off the roof was captured in tarps and whisked away daily, and the whole job only took three days because he sent a big enough crew to get the work done before the snow came.

I don't know if these geniuses are Christians, but they certainly embrace the Christian work ethic, and we're thankful we found them. They are part of our lives. Without them, life would be much more unpleasant and expensive.

> *Whatever you do, work at it with all your heart, as working for the Lord, not for men.* —Colossians 3:23

CHORES

I don't know how many children still have chores these days with the decline of the family farm and today's hectic pace, but there's something good to be said for them. We're talking about unpaid work here, not something done to earn an allowance but something done to contribute to the family's welfare. A child can be bribed to do anything, but that's not doing chores.

One of our sons was given the chore of doing some family laundry when I went back to work. If he didn't take his job seriously, everyone ran out of clean socks. Another set the table every night, or we couldn't sit down to eat. The third kept an eye on her youngest brother after school. They switched chores around now and then, but everyone had some responsibility for keeping the family running more or less smoothly.

None of them ever thought of chores as a blessing, but they were. Chores showed our children that they were a vital part of the family, that they counted and we were better off as a family because of their efforts. Chores gave them pride in doing a job properly and prepared them for the workplace. We didn't overload them—they rarely spent more than half an hour a day doing them—but chores taught our children a lot more than homework ever did.

> *Make it your ambition to lead a quiet life,*
> *to mind your own business and to work*
> *with your hands. . .so that your daily life*
> *may win the respect of outsiders and so that*
> *you will not be dependent on anybody.*
>
> —1 Thessalonians 4:11–12

REFLECTIONS

It was the last week of September, chilly but not yet cold in Maine, and we were in a canoe, lake fishing for landlocked salmon with no great success. Still, we fished diligently, concentrating on our rod tips and lines and blocking out all distractions, waiting for that elusive tap of the line that meant a salmon was exploring our bait.

Then the early morning sun broke out, and I let my attention wander to the mountains circling the lake. It was peak leaf season. Yellow and red with patches of fir green rioted up and down the hills, taking my breath away. The air was so clear that each leaf stood out in individual glory, the lake so calm that I couldn't tell where the forest ended and its reflection in the lake began. At first, my eyes strained to see the invisible shoreline. I knew it was there, but I could not pinpoint its location, and this vaguely bothered me. Then I gave up looking for reality and gave in to beauty.

This must be what heaven's like, I thought. Once I knew where the shoreline was, and it was wonderful in itself, but there was so much more I didn't understand beyond the shoreline, and it was even more beautiful.

> *Now we see but a poor reflection as in a mirror; then we shall see face to face. Now I know in part; then I shall know fully, even as I am fully known.*
>
> —1 Corinthians 13:12

LOONS

Nature can fool you. All my life I have loved loons, the sign of a healthy wilderness lake and abundant fish. Then one day a loon erupted under our canoe, slashing through the water like a torpedo and scaring me out of my peaceful fishing and floating.

"Oh, no!" muttered my guide. "He's back again."

The torpedo was a loon in full chase, remarkably streamlined and swift, gobbling up tiny trout without mercy. He circled our canoe like the predator he is until we gave up fishing, afraid we'd catch him or at least hinder the escape of his prey. My guide was furious that our fishing was done for the day.

"It's okay," I assured him. "I can catch fish anytime, but where else can I watch a loon work like this?" The shallow, glass-clear water gave us a perfect view of the loon's hunting. At times he used our canoe as a blind, hiding behind it, then striking out. I don't know how many trout the loon took that day, but it was certainly more than we took. Loons don't practice catch-and-release.

I no longer romanticize loons. They are supreme masters of fishing, swift and voracious, not just symbols of the wilderness. I don't love them any the less for this, but I do understand their character a little more fully, thanks to God's little lesson of the loon.

Which of all these does not know that the hand of the Lord has done this? In his hand is the life of every creature and the breath of all mankind. —Job 12:9–10

NICK

I've gone about as long as I can without talking about my grandchildren, who are, of course, perfect in every way. Nick is the eldest, our first grandchild, which means we will always be his willing slaves. He looks just like his mother and two uncles, so he will soon begin losing his hair while his father will forever have a full head of it. We would have preferred to lose that particular gene battle.

Nick is destined to be a diplomat. He's kind and cooperative, a peacemaker who loves everyone.

I'd advise both political parties to court him at a young age. The fact that he's nobody's fool may preclude a political career, however.

Gone are the days when he would jump out of the car and race into my arms. Now I have to hug him more discreetly, when none of his many friends are around to see, but he knows I need his hugs and suffers my affection gracefully.

Is he as perfect as I claim he is? Of course not. Do I give a fig? Of course not! He will carry on the good and bad characteristics of all his ancestors, hopefully more of the good and less of the bad. He's blessed my life, and I know he will bless the lives of many others to come.

Even a child is known by his actions, by whether his conduct is pure and right.

—Proverbs 20:11

ALLIE

Her mother only wanted to know whether her teachers called her Allison or Allie, so she asked, "What do they say in school when they call your name?"

" 'Allie, be quiet!' " the first grader replied.

That's our second grandchild—unfailingly honest, never afraid of speaking the truth. Allie does not suffer fools kindly, but she never means to hurt anyone. She knows what she knows and never sugarcoats her opinions. She speaks right up, usually loudly. Takes after me a little, you might say. Allie is not going to be a diplomat, but if sheer volume counts, she is going to be a leader. Fortunately she's got a great mind and an iron will, not to mention boundless enthusiasm. No one is ever going to walk all over this young woman; she'd take them right off at the knees for trying.

Despite all her strength, Allie is 100 percent female, preferring skirts over slacks and not above using her feminine wiles to change the mind of any male. It's hard to get a hug from her, though. First of all, she's a moving target. But when she wants to, she'll sort of lean against you like a puppy taking a break and let you tell her how special she is, a tiny smile of pleasure her reward for speaking what is obviously the truth. She's going to be a very interesting teenager!

"May the Lord make the woman who is coming into your home like Rachel and Leah, who together built up the house of Israel." —Ruth 4:11

CONFIDENCE

It's so easy to get ground down by circumstances to the point where we are unsure of everything and everyone. Who can we trust today? Huge corporations fail, taking our retirement savings with them and leaving the security of our old age in doubt. People from countries whose names we can't spell make targets of us for reasons we can't begin to fathom. Diseases once believed conquered reappear stronger than ever. Nothing is sure these days. At least that's how it feels.

Yet the Lord tells us, " 'And surely I am with you always, to the very end of the age' " (Matthew 28:20). " 'Do not be afraid. I am the First and the Last. I am the Living One; I was dead, and behold I am alive for ever and ever! And I hold the keys of death and Hades' " (Revelation 1:17–18).

Much of the time we must live with things the way they are because it is not in our power to change them, but when our confidence fails there is still someone we can cling to—the Lord who came to save us and loves us still. We may cling to Him in confidence, for He will never fail us. He is always there to lift us up again, to give us confidence and show us the path of love that leads us toward a hopeful future.

"For God so loved the world that he gave his one and only Son, that whoever believes in him shall not perish but have eternal life. For God did not send his Son into the world to condemn the world, but to save the world through him."

—John 3:16–17

THE REEF

We were aboard a seaworthy fishing boat on our way to some reef fishing—my husband, myself, and our two teenaged boys. Unfortunately, before you can fish the reef you have to go through it. The passageway was narrow and the waves horrendous, pouring over our bow and slamming it down with a thud as we tried to make progress against them. Half of the time the prop was not even in the water, just churning the air above a wave.

We huddled in the lee of the pilothouse for protection, encased in our life preservers. I, the worst of all flyers, was doing fine—not a touch of seasickness. One son was silent and frightened; the other was green—actually, literally green. My husband was laughing.

Standing next to us, a crew member watched us carefully and provided progress reports. "We're okay. You okay?" She looked dubiously at our green son and kicked a bucket closer to his feet. "All right, here comes the big one. Hang on." One more shudder, one more shower, one more slam, and it all stopped. The prop caught hold of the sea and drove us into a perfectly sunny, dry day.

I don't think we caught one fish that day, but no one cared. We had survived the sea's fury; dry land was in sight, and going through the passage on the way home was like being shot from a slingshot because the waves were, for once, working for us. And I thought reef fishing would be calmer than going further out to sea!

Mightier than the thunder of the great waters, mightier than the breakers of the sea—the Lord on high is mighty.

—Psalm 93:4

SERVING THE OUTCAST

When our children were teenagers, we told them to pick their friends carefully because other people would judge them by the friends they kept. They thought that was ridiculous and unfair, but they eventually learned it was true—sometimes the hard way. Of course it was unfair, and I give them credit for seeing and resenting that, but even Jesus was socially censured for associating with tax collectors, the sick, and sinners of poor reputation. That was where His work was, and no amount of tongue-wagging was about to hinder His ministry to society's outcasts.

Not all of us can be as committed to serving the outcast; none of us have Jesus' gumption. We prefer to have friends who resemble us to some extent, friends who are upstanding church members, pillars of society, so to say. We identify with them and want to be like them. When we do good works for society's outcasts, we can hardly wait to catch the next bus home, where we feel comfortable and secure. This does not make us bad people, only humans with understandable concerns. The blessing comes to us when we gather our courage and step out in faith to do the Lord's work, wherever it takes us. Volunteering to work at a shelter will not change the world, but it will change us. Perhaps that is the whole point.

"The blind receive sight, the lame walk, those who have leprosy are cured, the deaf hear, the dead are raised, and the good news is preached to the poor." —Matthew 11:5

HUMPBACKS

It was time for dinner on the cruise ship, but no one went down to eat because it was also dinnertime for the humpback whales off our bow. You couldn't begin to count them. Every time someone came up with a number, there would be new spouts circling the horizon. We were literally surrounded. No more than ten feet off our port, a mother and her baby dove shallow, surfaced, and rested, keeping their distance from the main feast.

We watched two or three whales dive and

circle, enclosing their meal-to-be in a bubble net that rose slowly from below and erupted in a silver shower when the whales surfaced with their mouths wide open, gulping hundreds of fish in one swallow. Their ancestors had been netting fish this way long before mankind tied its first knot on its first net. Others flung themselves to the water in what we would call a belly flop, stunning the fish beneath them and scooping them up. The water around us was in constant motion, although farther away it was calm as a lake.

The pod moved as it fed, and we kept our position among them, the mother and baby hovering near us while we traveled. The mist from their blowholes drifted over our faces, surprisingly warm on our cheeks. Soon it was over, the bait fish either gone or devoured. The pod dove and swam off, the mother and baby with them, and we went below to our own waiting dinner.

"But ask the animals, and they will teach you. . .or let the fish of the sea inform you. Which of these does not know that the hand of the Lord has done this?"

—Job 12:7–9

HOUSE CLEANING

I discovered long ago that I was not good at cleaning. Some people actually enjoy it, but I found it as rewarding as having teeth pulled. The problem is, you are never done with it, never satisfied that you captured every last dust bunny or swept away every cookie crumb. Even if you did, more would begin to accumulate before you put away the mop. Cleaning has a certain built-in futility.

But I did it for a good twenty years as the children grew up, and nobody ever caught a horrible disease from the cobwebs I knew I missed. When I went back to work and collected my first pitiful paycheck, it finally dawned on me that I could pay other people to clean my house. My mother had never had help, even though she worked all her life, but she was a better woman than I am, or at least less compulsive.

Ever since then I've had a crew of people who appear every week and accomplish more in one hour than I could by cleaning every spare second of my day. I still have to do some cleaning, but the burden is off my back. Help arrives every Wednesday afternoon, regular as clockwork, and I don't go looking for trouble in corners or anywhere else. To me this is the abundant life in spades.

For he will deliver the needy who cry out,
the afflicted who have no one to help.

—Psalm 72:12

DYSLEXIA

Somewhere in the second grade, one of our sons went through the process of not learning to read. Everyone else in his class was doing fine, but not him. People (even teachers!) called him stupid and lazy, although we knew he was neither. He was a third generation dyslexic—perhaps fourth or fifth generation, for all we know. I cannot begin to imagine what he went through that year, especially when we began to listen to the "experts" who thought he was somehow lacking or responsible for his own "failure." Finally we put our trust in our child and made such a racket that the school tested him, confirmed our diagnosis, and provided the help he needed. Today it would not take a whole school year to spot this problem, and I hope no school would think to blame the victim.

Now our son reads for pleasure, although he reads slowly. He graduated from college and is quite successful in a demanding position, thanks to a trained teacher who believed in him and showed him how to navigate through a world of letters that once made no sense to him. Sometimes the system fails children, and when it does, sometimes parents listen to the system instead of the child. Don't be afraid to disagree with a teacher and make a pest of yourself, because if your child can't depend on you, who on earth can he look to for help?

They cried to you and were saved; in you they trusted and were not disappointed.

—Psalm 22:5

GIFTS

I used to take great pleasure in going out to the toy store and buying gifts for my children. I knew what they would love and what they would ignore, so it was fun, and my gifts were always right on the mark. Now that they are grown, I have no idea what to buy them, so I take the easy way out and send a card with a check.

I do this because my grandson once told me that the best gift I could give him was cash. He knew exactly what he wanted and would be able to buy a great present if everyone just gave him money. I figured that if that pleased him, it probably would also please his mother and uncles. Still I felt a little guilty, so I bought the best card I could find to hold the check, cards that said how much I appreciated and loved them, only to see my grandson rip into the card to get to the cash. Any card would do, as long as his name was on the envelope.

Then last Christmas, one son gave me a bookstore gift certificate. I admit it didn't knock me over on Christmas Day, but once the holiday was past, I took the certificate and spent a lot of time looking through the shelves until I located five paperback books I really wanted to read but had never bought for myself. It was wonderful! I no longer feel in the least guilty about passing out checks instead of gifts.

> *"If you, then, though you are evil, know*
> *how to give good gifts to your children, how*
> *much more will your Father in heaven give*
> *good gifts to those who ask him!"*
>
> —Matthew 7:11

HOUSES

There is a shortage of houses for sale in our area. "We're low on inventory," as my friend the Realtor says, as though houses were cardboard cartons or duct tape. We even got a telephone call from a Realtor who swore she had a buyer for our house, which is not on the market. I could not believe she had actually driven some clients past our house and gotten an offer. No one's that stupid. I was tempted to ask what she could sell this unremarkable house for (which was obviously the preferred response) but realized that if the offer was too good to turn down, we would soon be the clients cruising by houses that were not for sale.

Worse yet, we would have to move. Do you have any idea how much junk a pack rat husband can accumulate in a one-car garage? Moving does not motivate him to ditch the junk (I tried that once) but to pack it carefully and fill up a new garage with the old junk. The last time we moved we filled up two moving vans, one of which could have been totally destroyed and still have left us with more than enough stuff to fill up a house. So no thank you, everybody; our house is not for sale. We intend to retire right here and leave the mess for our children to divide or (finally) throw away.

Selling their possessions and goods, they gave to anyone as he had need.

—Acts 2:45

TRADITIONS

When we were young and strong and our house was filled with little children, we were great tradition makers. We borrowed them from my husband's family and my family and even made up our own. The Easter egg hunt had detailed rules and regulations; the Christmas tree was decorated with candy canes to be shared with all guests. On Thanksgiving we ate turkey; at Christmas, roast beef and Yorkshire pudding. Before we knew it, we had completely filled every holiday with traditions that could not be varied in the least. The kids loved it.

Tradition did make every holiday special. It also made every holiday somewhat of a burden, especially if someone forgot to buy the candy canes and all the stores were closed. Let me tell you, finding Easter candy at 9:00 P.M. on Easter eve while on vacation in Florida was not easy, either (they made do with M&Ms). Then there was the Easter that everyone arrived here for dinner without letting me know they were coming, and I only had two lamb chops in the refrigerator. We had Chinese food.

One day I reached my breaking point—I think it was the Chinese food for Easter dinner. They were all grown adults. I told them they were on their own. They were free to pirate any tradition they chose. Failing that, they could make their own traditions. I personally enjoyed eating Chinese food for Easter—but I refuse to make it a tradition!

I was. . .extremely zealous for the traditions of my fathers.

—Galatians 1:14

CAREERS

If you had asked me when I was eight what I wanted to be when I grew up, I would have said I wanted to be a newspaper reporter—a foreign correspondent, to be precise. During high school and college I actually did some local reporting. It was fun, but I soon learned that shy people aren't suited for interviewing strangers every day.

I had my first poem published when I was in college, then a short story. No big deal. Then I opted for marriage and motherhood, which paid poorly but had great fringe benefits. A local publisher advertised for an editor when my children were in their teens, and somehow I got the job. After working in editorial and marketing departments for several years, I went freelance, editing and writing, where I am today.

I tell you all this because it's a relatively straight career line, one I never could have imagined for myself at the age of eight, when I figured I had no chance of fulfilling my childhood ambitions. I could not see a plan in the various jobs I had, but I have no doubt God had one and kept steering until I got where I was meant to be. I don't want to be a foreign correspondent anymore—at least not very often.

> *I will instruct you and teach you in the*
> *way you should go; I will counsel you and*
> *watch over you.* —Psalm 32:8

AUTHOR BIO

Toni Sortor is a freelance writer and editor in suburban New York. She has cowritten several Barbour books, including *The Word on Life, Prayers and Promises,* and *Daily Wisdom for Couples.*